Interactive Study Guide for the

TExES Pedagogy and Professional Responsibilities Tests

NANCY J. HADLEY
Angelo State University

MARILYN J. EISENWINE
Angelo State University

PEARSON

Boston   New York   San Francisco   Mexico City   Montreal
Toronto   London   Madrid   Munich   Paris   Hong Kong
Singapore   Tokyo   Cape Town   Sydney

Executive Editor and Publisher: *Stephen D. Dragin*
Series Editorial Assistant: *Kate Heimsoth*
Marketing Manager: *Weslie Sellinger*
Production Editor: *Paula Carroll*
Editorial Production Service: *Publishers' Design and Production Services, Inc.*
Composition Buyer: *Linda Cox*
Manufacturing Buyer: *Linda Morris*
Electronic Composition: *Publishers' Design and Production Services, Inc.*
Interior Design: *Publishers' Design and Production Services, Inc.*
Cover Administrator: *Elena Sidorova*

For related titles and support materials, visit our online catalog at www.ablongman.com.

Between the time website information is gathered and then published, it is not unusual for some sites to have closed. Also, the transcription of URLs can result in typographical errors. The publisher would appreciate notification where these errors occur so that they may be corrected in subsequent editions.

Cataloging-in-Publication data unavailable at press time.

ISBN 10: 0-205-50354-3
ISBN 13: 978-0-205-50354-4

Printed in the United States of America

10 9 8 7 6 5 4 3 2 1   CIN   11 10 09 08 07

*The authors would like to dedicate this publication
to their husbands and children
for their love and support.*

About the Authors

Nancy J. Hadley is an associate professor in the Department of Curriculum and Instruction at Angelo State University in San Angelo, Texas. She has a B.S. from the University of Texas at Austin, a M.Ed. from Angelo State University and a Ed.D. from the University of North Texas. She served as a computer programmer/analyst, a technology consultant/instructor as well as a secondary mathematics teacher before joining the Angelo State University faculty. Her research interests include prerequisites for digital learning, empowering curriculum development, and technology integration.

Marilyn J. Eisenwine is an associate professor in the Department of Teacher Education at Angelo State University in San Angelo, Texas. She has a B.S. and M.Ed. from Texas Tech University, and a Ph.D. from the University of Texas at Austin. Previously, she taught for 25 years in Texas public schools, including seven years as a Reading Recovery® teacher. Her research interests include literacy acquisition, technology integration, and archaeology education.

Contents

Preface   ix

1   TEST PHILOSOPHY   1

Learner-Centered Proficiencies for Teachers   1
Philosophy Exercise   5

2   TEST-TAKING STRATEGIES   7

Rules of the Game   7
Question Dissection Exercise   10

3   INDISPENSABLE INFORMATION   15

General Vocabulary   15
General Vocabulary Exercise   17
Flashcard Exercise   19
Research-Based Practices   20
Research-Based Exercise   22
Dos and Don'ts   24
Dos and Don'ts Exercise   25
Word Associations   26
Word Association Exercise   27
Common Verbs   28
Common Verb Exercise   29

4   DOMAIN I   31

Vocabulary   32

Vocabulary Exercise   34

Content   36

Content Exercise   47

5   DOMAIN II   49

Vocabulary   50

Vocabulary Exercise   51

Content   52

Content Exercise   57

6   DOMAIN III   59

Vocabulary   61

Vocabulary Exercise   62

Content   63

Content Exercise   78

7   DOMAIN IV   81

Vocabulary   82

Vocabulary Exercise   83

Content   84

Content Exercise   97

8   FINAL EXERCISES   99

Abbreviations Exercise   99

Practice Test Analysis Exercise   101

Synthesis Exercise   102

EXERCISE ANSWER KEYS   107

General Vocabulary Exercise   107

Research-Based Practices Exercise   107

Dos and Don'ts Exercise   108

Word Association Exercise   108

Common Verbs Exercise   108

Vocabulary Exercises   109

APPENDICES
Appendix A: Competency Charts   111

Appendix B: Practice Test Analysis Charts   127

Index   141

Preface

WHAT

The Texas State Board for Educator Certification (SBEC) has specified pedagogy and professional standards for Texas educators. These standards form the basis for the Texas Examinations of Educator Standards (TExES), which are part of the licensure tests for teachers in Texas. The content covered by these tests is organized into areas called domains. Each domain covers a specific area of educator standards. Within each domain, the content is broken down into a set of competencies. The Pedagogy and Professional Responsibilities (PPR) tests for certification include thirteen competencies.

This study guide prepares students to take any of the PPR certification exams. It is essential that students master the content of the standards.

Standards-based tests present a formidable hurdle, not because test-takers have failed to master the content, but because the tests are presented in a multiple-choice maze that often misleads the test-taker. The TExES tests require students to practice critical thinking skills in applying knowledge of the standards to classroom situations presented. Students, particularly at-risk students, get lost in the labyrinth of verbiage presented in the standards, test frameworks, and competencies. These students have difficulty making decisions concerning standards and content in an intimidating, high-stakes environment. This study guide offers an interactive approach targeting students who have not been successful using more traditional test-preparation materials.

In many cases, it is not that the student has failed to master the required content; it is that the student is unable to maneuver the intent of the question. The traditional preparation approach of learning facts, interpreting these facts, and then applying them in the test situation is no longer enough to ensure success on this type of test. The test-takers must not only have a mastery of the facts but must learn how to be successful on a decision-making test regarding classroom scenarios presented in the questions. This study guide highlights the most critical information through an innovative bold and bulleted approach. The authors model techniques for determining the question asked and how to make the best choice for answering that specific question. Students become empowered by active engagement in constructivist activities that focus on key content and test-taking strategies.

WHY

The authors believe that the major difficulty students have in passing the TExES is trying to sift through the volume of information to which they have been exposed and determine which piece of information is pertinent to answering a complex question. Condensing key concepts for students entails emphasizing words with bold typeface and shortening content into bulleted phrases.

The senior author has analyzed both ExCET (Examination for the Certification of Educators in Texas) and TExES practice test questions for a number of years to isolate pertinent content and develop test-taking strategies geared toward struggling students. While utilizing other test preparation materials over a ten-year period in teacher preparation courses, she became frustrated with the volume of information overwhelming students. To provide more specific test review information, the professor discovered that backloading curriculum by aligning the test with targeted materials produced a more effective test preparation tool.[1] In the process of constantly field testing methodology and interviewing students who "just don't get it," the senior author has refined the tactics presented in this study guide. Data collected in a pilot study with students using study guide materials indicated an average gain of over 10 percent and a maximum gain of over 40 percent between practice tests.

Statistics also indicate that after failing the actual TExES exam for the first time, a downward spiral occurs for the student. The number of times this student must take the test in order to pass increases inordinately. After taking the test, students are not informed as to specific questions missed, so they do not know which questions they answered correctly and which questions they answered incorrectly. Furthermore, they may encounter the exact same questions on subsequent exams. Multiple test-takers begin to recognize test scenarios and answer choices. Struggling students become confused as to how they should answer correctly. Naturally, their self-esteem and confidence decline. In order to avoid this downward spiral, the student must be actively engaged with condensed content and test-taking strategies before encountering the test for the first time.

---

[1]Betty E. Steffy and Fenwick W. English, *Curriculum and Assessment for World-Class Schools* (Lancaster, PA: Technomic Publishing Company, 1997).

For students to be successful with standardized testing, they must make connections between their knowledge of the standards and the test. Even students who are able to memorize test content are often unable to make necessary connections when answering test questions. Past experiences of the authors in helping students pass certification exams have indicated that active engagement helps them make critical connections. These connections are facilitated through constructivist experiences. Concerning constructivist experiences, Callahan, Clark, and Kellough note that students build their knowledge not from "previously established steps" but by "student manipulation" of curriculum materials.[2] The authors have included successful activities that actively engage students in construction of their own knowledge resulting in improved test scores. This study guide contains a compilation of constructivist experiences for students and test-taking strategies that assist students in organizing knowledge of the standards and competencies into a form that can be applied to the question stems presented on the TExES. This active approach results in the empowerment of the students in making the necessary connections between knowledge and test-taking skills.

WHO

These materials may be used by individuals or within a classroom setting. Individuals may work through the activities at their own pace, reinforcing their knowledge base with the strategies they need to successfully navigate the maze of test questions. When utilized in a classroom environment, social collaboration helps students capitalize on constructivist interaction. According to Vygotsky, "With appropriate challenges and assistance from teachers or more capable peers, students are moved forward into their zone of proximal development where new learning occurs."[3] Whether used individually or as a course textbook, the authors have designed the materials in this study guide to increase student ownership in the learning process.

HOW

This book provides the necessary condensed version of test content or a shortcut in bold and bulleted format. The simplified format has proven helpful in preparing all students to successfully sift through the volume of information necessary to pass the test. Unabridged resources often over-

[2]Joseph F. Callahan, Leonard H. Clark, and Richard D. Kellough, *Teaching in the Middle and Secondary Schools* (Englewood, NJ: Merrill/Prentice Hall, 1995), p. 17.

[3]Arends, R., *Learning to Teach* (Boston: McGraw Hill, 1998), p. 353.

whelm students, especially at-risk students, with too much detail. This booklet condenses related content into a manageable outline format and delineates question dissection strategies that are specifically designed for multiple-choice tests. To be successful, the student must be able to recall targeted content in response to dissected question stems, while avoiding carefully constructed distracters, thus revealing the correct answer. This study guide offers multiple approaches and outlines key content while increasing ownership in the learning process.

The proven methodology presented in this booklet progresses through content and activities in a prescribed sequence. Initially, students must understand and embrace the philosophy underlying the test. Next, they must master such indispensable information as question dissection, research-based practices, and word associations. Then, students internalize vocabulary and competencies in manageable amounts, reinforced through activities and exercises throughout the study guide. The above components comprise a successful methodology presented by the authors in a bold and bulleted format that develops the necessary mindset for success on the TExES tests.

ACKNOWLEDGMENTS

We would like to thank the following reviewers for their time and input:
Candy Combs Skelton, Texas A&M University, Corpus Christi; Carol H. Thomas, Texas Woman's University; and Janet Whitley, Tarleton State University.

1

Test Philosophy

In the early 1990s, the **Texas Education Agency (TEA)** launched a major initiative to restructure the education profession through a comprehensive and coherent professional development system. The purpose of the initiative was to incorporate a central vision for preparing students for the twenty-first century while fostering excellence and equity for all children. As a result of this initiative, the state adopted *Learner-Centered Schools for Texas: A Vision of Texas Educators*, a set of proficiencies that teachers and administrators must possess and be able to demonstrate to provide all children in Texas with access to a quality education.[1] The Pedagogy and Professional Responsibilities (PPR) TExES exams, as part of the teacher certification process, are based on Learner-Centered Proficiencies comprising a philosophy students must embrace in order to be successful.

LEARNER-CENTERED PROFICIENCIES FOR TEACHERS

The Learner-Centered Proficiencies for teachers in Texas consist of:

- Learner-Centered Knowledge
- Learner-Centered Instruction
- Equity and Excellence for All Learners
- Learner-Centered Communication
- Learner-Centered Professional Development

[1]Texas Education Agency, *Learner-Centered Schools for Texas: A Vision of Texas Educators*, (Austin, Texas, February, 1994) GE4 204 02.

The language of the PPR TExES exam sometimes includes **exact wording** from these Learner-Centered Proficiencies. **Recognizing** and **understanding** these phrases help test-takers adopt the **appropriate classroom philosophy,** as well as make critical decisions in choosing correct answers on the exam.

Learner-Centered Knowledge

The teacher possesses and draws on a rich knowledge base of content, pedagogy, and technology to provide relevant and meaningful learning experiences for all students.

The teacher exhibits a strong working knowledge of subject matter and enables students to better understand patterns of thinking specific to a discipline.

The teacher stays abreast of **current knowledge and practice** within the content area, related disciplines, and technology; participates in **professional development activities;** and **collaborates** with other professionals. Moreover, the teacher contributes to the knowledge base and understands the pedagogy of the discipline.

As the teacher guides learners to construct knowledge through experiences, they learn about relationships among and within the **central themes** of various disciplines while also learning **how to learn.** Recognizing the dynamic nature of knowledge, the teacher selects and organizes topics so students make **clear connections** between what is taught in the classroom and what they experience outside the classroom. As students probe these relationships, the teacher encourages **discussion** in which both the teacher's and the students' opinions are valued. To further develop multiple perspectives, the teacher **integrates** other disciplines, learners' interests, and technological resources so that learners consider the central themes of the subject matter from as many **different cultural and intellectual viewpoints** as possible.

Learner-Centered Instruction

To create a learner-centered community, the teacher collaboratively identifies needs; and plans, implements, and assesses instruction using technology and other resources.

The teacher is a leader of a **learner-centered community,** in which an atmosphere of trust and openness produces a stimulating exchange of ideas and mutual respect. The **teacher** is a **critical thinker** and **problem solver** who plays a variety of roles when teaching. As a **coach,** the teacher observes, evaluates, and changes directions and strategies whenever necessary. As a **facilitator,** the teacher helps students link ideas in the content area to familiar ideas, to prior experiences, and to relevant problems. As a **manager,** the teacher effectively acquires, allocates, and conserves resources. By **encouraging self-directed learning** and by **modeling respectful behavior,** the teacher effectively manages the learning environment so that optimal learning occurs.

Assessment is used to guide the learner community. By using assessment as an integral part of instruction, the teacher responds to the needs of all learners. In addition, the teacher guides learners to develop personally meaningful forms of **self-assessment.**

The teacher selects materials, technology, activities, and space that are developmentally appropriate and designed to engage interest in learning. As a result, learners work independently and cooperatively in a positive and stimulating learning climate fueled by self-discipline and motivation.

Although the teacher has a vision of the destination of learning, **students set individual goals and plan** how to reach the destination. As a result, they **take responsibility** for their own learning, develop a sense of the importance of learning for understanding, and begin to understand themselves as learners. The teacher's plans integrate learning experiences and various forms of assessment that take into consideration the unique characteristics of the learner community. The teacher shares responsibility for the results of this process with all members of the learning community.

Together, learners and teachers **take risks** in trying out innovative ideas for learning. To facilitate learning, the teacher encourages various types of learners to shape their own learning through active engagement, manipulation, and examination of ideas and materials. **Critical thinking, creativity,** and **problem solving** spark further learning. Consequently, there is an appreciation of **learning as a life-long process** that builds a greater understanding of the world and a feeling of responsibility toward it.

Equity in Excellence for All Learners

The teacher responds appropriately to diverse groups of learners.

The teacher not only respects and is **sensitive to all learners** but also encourages the use of all their skills and talents. As the facilitator of learning, the teacher models and encourages appreciation for students' **cultural heritage, unique endowments, learning styles, interests,** and **needs.** The teacher also designs learning experiences that show consideration for these student characteristics.

Because the teacher views differences as opportunities for learning, **cross-cultural experiences** are an integral part of the learner-centered community. In addition, the teacher establishes a relationship between the curriculum and community cultures. While making this connection, the teacher and students explore attitudes that foster unity. As a result, the teacher creates an environment in which learners **work cooperatively** and purposefully use a variety of resources to understand themselves, their immediate community, and the **global society** in which they live.

Learner-Centered Communication

While acting as an advocate for all students and the school, the teacher demonstrates effective professional and interpersonal communication skills.

As a leader, the teacher **communicates the mission of the school** with learners, professionals, families, and community members. With colleagues, the teacher works to create an environment in which taking risks, sharing new ideas, and innovative problem solving are supported and encouraged. With citizens, the teacher works to establish strong and **positive ties between the school and the community.**

Because the teacher is a compelling communicator, students begin to appreciate the importance of expressing their views clearly. The teacher uses **verbal, nonverbal,** and **media** techniques so that students explore ideas collaboratively, pose questions, and support one another in their learning. The teacher and students listen, speak, read, and write in a variety of contexts; give multimedia and artistic presentations; and use technology as a resource for building communication skills. The teacher incorporates techniques of **inquiry** that enable students to use different levels of thinking.

The teacher also communicates effectively as an advocate for each learner. The teacher is sensitive to concerns that affect learners and takes advantage of community strengths and resources for the learners' welfare.

Learner-Centered Professional Development

The teacher as a reflective practitioner dedicated to all students' success demonstrates a commitment to learn, to improve the profession, and to maintain professional ethics and personal integrity.

As a learner, the teacher works within a framework of clearly defined **professional goals** to plan for and profit from a wide variety of relevant learning opportunities. The teacher develops an identity as a professional, interacts effectively with colleagues, and takes a role in setting standards for teacher accountability. In addition, the teacher uses **technological and other resources** to facilitate continual professional growth.

To strengthen the effectiveness and quality of teaching, the teacher actively engages in an exchange of ideas with colleagues, observes peers, and encourages feedback from learners to establish a successful learning community. As a member of a **collaborative team,** the teacher identifies and uses group processes to make decisions and solve problems.

The teacher exhibits the highest standard of professionalism and bases daily decisions on **ethical principles.** To support the needs of learners, the teacher knows and uses community resources, school services, and laws relating to teacher responsibilities and student rights. Through these activities, the teacher contributes to the improvement of comprehensive educational programs as well as programs within specific disciplines.

PHILOSOPHY EXERCISE

Test-takers must be able to clearly identify the philosophy behind the TExES exam. This philosophy is based on the Learner-Centered Proficiencies for Teachers in Texas. In order to pick out correct answers, test-takers **must** recognize what answers the philosophy would support and eliminate answers it would not support. To internalize this philosophy, carefully read and study the Learner-Centered Proficiencies, then summarize each in Table 1.1. Next, brainstorm what a teacher would do and not do based each summary, recording in the table as well. For example, *Do* connect new knowledge to previous knowledge; *Don't* teach isolated skills. **If you cannot understand and apply this philosophy to the test questions, you will not pass the test.**

TABLE 1.1

Learner-Centered Knowledge (Summary)	*Example:*
	Do stay up to date on subject content.
	Don't use same lesson plans every year.
	Do
	Don't
	Do
	Don't
Learner-Centered Instruction (Summary)	*Example:*
	Do promote exchange of ideas.
	Don't use your own perspective only.
	Do
	Don't
	Do
	Don't

TABLE 1.1   *Continued*

Equity in Excellence for All Learners (Summary)	*Example:* *Do* highlight students' cultural heritage. *Don't* give examples from only one cultural group. *Do* *Don't* *Do* *Don't*
Learner-Centered Communication (Summary)	*Example:* *Do* use multimedia in the classroom. *Don't* use only the overhead projector. *Do* *Don't* *Do* *Don't*
Learner-Centered Professional Development (Summary)	*Example:* *Do* exchange ideas with other teachers. *Don't* isolate yourself in your room. *Do* *Don't* *Do* *Don't*

CHAPTER

2

Test-Taking Strategies

Popular opinion holds that a valid multiple-choice test requires critical thinking. Test-takers must demonstrate decision-making skills to prove they can think critically using content knowledge applied to test scenarios. Some test-takers are easily diverted and tempted to fall for the distracters when excessive verbiage prevents clear focus on the question. It is **essential** to know the principles and philosophies behind the test and be **skillful** in pinpointing the intent of the question.

Details not germane to the question often distract test-takers and lead them in a direction away from the question. For example, try this exercise:

> Say *joke*. Say *joke* two times. Say *joke* three times. Say *joke* four times. What is the white of the egg called?

If you answered *yolk*, you were thinking in one direction due to the momentum of repeating the word *joke*. The answer to the question is simply *egg white*. This is how easy it is to be misled and miss the intent of the question. In this manner the details in the test scenarios relating to practical school situations can lead the test-taker to an answer that is correct for the situation but does not directly answer the question.

RULES OF THE GAME

1. *First read and understand the question or the statement to complete.* Because the multiple-choice game is a game of words, it is important **focus on the question** being asked. Start by **underlining** the question

or the last sentence just before the answers. Sometimes it is a statement to complete and is not posed as a question, such as "The *most likely* result will be . . . ," or "The teacher should take into consideration all of the following factors *except*. . . ." For purposes of this study guide the term "question" should be interpreted to mean either question or statement to complete. Read to understand the question and focus on what the question is asking.

2. ***Identify any keywords in the question.*** Keywords are significant words that convey intent and narrow the focus. For example, *most likely* and *except* in the samples on Rule 1 are keywords. Identify keywords like *best, most, likely, first, appropriate, unlikely, not, except, disadvantage,* and *primarily.* Circle these words. If the question involves picking the *best* answer, there will probably be at least two good answers, but the tricky part is that only one is the *best* match for the question. Reread the question to determine the best match. If the question requires picking the *first* step, all of the answers will be appropriate, so be sure to pick the one that should be done *first* in the sequence of steps. Spend time determining **exactly** what the question is asking before you continue.

    If the question has the words *approach, principle,* or *strategy* in the question, it is typically a generic (general) question and does not have anything to do with the specifics of the scenario. Many times the distracting answers apply to the scenario and are reasonable teaching practices for this specific situation. The important thing is to pick the answer that is an *approach, principle,* or *strategy,* even though this general answer seems out of place among more specific choices directly related to the scenario.

3. ***Eliminate distracters and identify potentially correct answers.*** Read the answers and cross through any obviously wrong answers and circle the good possibilities. Watch for answers that **draw your attention away** from the intent of the question. These **distracters** could be good educational practices in the situation posed but do not directly answer the question. Some answers are opposed to the good teaching practices exemplified by the Learner-Centered Philosophy. You can cross out those answers immediately.

4. ***When you are struggling between two answers, reread the question.*** When selecting between two possible answers, make sure to reread the question in order to determine exactly what the question is asking. If the question is difficult to understand, **rewrite** it in your own words in the margin of the test. **Making sure to select the choice that directly answers the question is the critical step.** Caution: Do not read more into the question than is stated. A common mistake is to select an answer that would be an end result of the steps taken in the situa-

tion rather than the answer that correlates directly with the question posed. If you have to rationalize the answer, it is not a correct answer. You are overthinking it!

5. *Identify the verbs in the answers if you are still unsure.* Many times the correct answer surfaces by examining all of the **verbs** in the answers. For example, when the question concerns the *first step* in a planning process and verb choices are *schedule, meet, analyze,* or *work,* consider the answer containing *analyze,* because the first step in planning anything is to analyze the data or situation.

6. *Make sure you understand the intent of the entire answer.* Do not pick an answer that merely sounds good. If you do not fully understand the complete intent of the answer, it is probably a wrong answer. Remember that the test-maker must write a question with a clear answer and that distracters can be written with muddled meanings. Often good practices are combined with poor practices in one answer. In addition, good phrases can be combined in confusing ways to produce wrong answers. Sometimes answers contain more than one part. **Read the full answer** before selecting the best choice. One answer may contain an **acceptable** part at the beginning but also an **unacceptable** practice near the end. Both parts of the answer must be **entirely correct.** For example, the following answer pertains to planning instruction:

> **Plan different versions** of lesson activities, and use **each one** with the **whole class every year.**

Notice the first part of this answer is correct because teachers should plan different versions of lesson activities. However, the last part of the answer is **NOT** correct because lessons should be designed to address the needs of individual students (individualized instruction) and not taught to the whole class as a general rule. In addition, teachers should **NOT** be using the same lesson plans year after year. Be sure to read **all the way to the end.** Don't be misled by your impression of the answer gleaned from the first few words.

7. *Apply the Learner-Centered Philosophy.* Because the Pedagogy and Professional Responsibilities exams are based on Learner-Centered Proficiencies, **always** consider this philosophy to choose an answer:

- That is **student-centered.**
- That allows students to **learn from their mistakes.**
- That promotes **higher level thinking skills.**
- That includes **discovery** and **cooperative learning.**
- That **celebrates diversity.**

- That encourages **heterogeneous grouping.**
- That promotes a **safe and orderly environment.**
- That **doesn't restrict special education students** any more than necessary.
- That is **age appropriate.**
- That follows the **chain of command.**

Remember to play the multiple-choice game by detecting correct answers based on the intent of the question and the underlying philosophy of the test. **If all answers are learner-centered, you must choose the one that directly answers the question.**

QUESTION DISSECTION EXERCISE

Refer to the following steps listed under **Rules of the Game** to analyze the practice questions in this exercise:

Step 1.   Read, understand, and **underline the question.**

You should spend most of your time on this step to determine **what the question is asking.** The correct answer will be the answer that is most closely aligned with the **intent** of the question.

Step 2.   **Circle keywords** in the question.

Remember, keywords are significant words that **convey intent** and narrow the focus.

Step 3.   Read all answers, **cross out distracters,** and **circle possible correct choices.**

Draw a line through any answers not directly aligned with the Learner-Centered Philosophy of the test. Remember to eliminate answers not relating to the **intent** of the question.

If you are still unsure continue.

Step 4.   If you are struggling between two answers, reread and **write the question** in the margin in your own words.

When given more than one learner-centered answer, many times the distracters address an end result, not the specific result identified in the question.

Use the above steps to analyze the following sample questions.

QUESTION 1.

Sally Jones is a new physical education teacher. She is planning for her coed classes, each of which is expected to include about 40 students. In planning instructional activities for the coming year, Ms. Jones should take into consideration all of the following factors except:

A. state curriculum guidelines.

B. students' daily academic schedules.

C. learners' needs and interests.

D. available equipment and space.

You should have circled the keyword *except* in the question. In this question you are looking for a wrong answer. Because you should always consider state guidelines and learners' needs, both A and C are correct. You can't plan anything without the equipment or the space so D is correct. The remaining answer concerning academic scheduling is a decision made by the principal, not the physical education teacher, so B is the answer.

QUESTION 2.

In discussing the coming school year with her mentor, a teacher with many years of experience, Ms. Gonzales decides to develop a set of goals for herself with regard to teaching her classes. After giving the matter some careful thought, she develops the following list.

FIGURE 2.1

1. Be enthusiastic and positive.
2. Communicate goals of activities to students.
3. Give clear, concise directions.
4. Keep to a minimum the time spent explaining activities to the entire class.
5. Learn all students' names as soon as possible and address them by name.
6. Establish clear behavior guidelines.

Ms. Gonzales is aware that it will be difficult for her to accomplish goal 5,

but she believes it is important for her to do so. The most likely result of her

accomplishing this goal will be to:

   A. enhance students' sense of self-worth within the class.

   B. encourage student adherence to established behavior guidelines.

   C. promote increased cooperation among students in the class.

   D. prompt students to apply higher standards in judging their own
       success.

The question is—What is the most likely result of the teacher's accomplishing this goal? You must look in the previous sentence to see that the goal is goal 5, learning all students' names and addressing them by name as soon as possible. Reading through the answers, you can cross out C and D because they have nothing to do with learning students' names and addressing students by their names. In this question you must stick with the exact question and not read anything else into the question.

Reread the question—you must find the answer that is the most likely, direct result of calling students by their names. Now if you are struggling between A and B, notice that goal 6 deals with behavior guidelines, not goal 5. If you selected B, you fell for the fake and were distracted with goal 6. In addition, B is common practice for teachers to do when they are correcting behavior. The answer is A—enhancing self-worth of students is the direct result of calling students by their names.

QUESTION 3.

Ms. Schmidt tells Mr. Alaniz she is concerned about students' lack of interest

in history class. Mr. Alaniz suggests that Ms. Schmidt have students brain-

storm on interesting historical personalities then select a personality for re-

search. He also recommends utilizing a wide range of traditional materials

as well as technology resources such as the Internet. The approach of pro-

viding students with a choice is most likely to help students to become self-

motivated by:

A. fostering their development of independent research skills.

B. stimulating their curiosity about historical personalities.

C. promoting a sense of ownership in their investigations.

D. increasing their willingness to participate for the sake of utilizing the Internet.

This is a question that contains the word *approach.* Remember, the words *approach, principle,* and *strategy* signify a generic answer. This is a general question that is not related to research, historical personalities, or the Internet included in the scenario as well as in answers A (research), B (historical personalities), and D (the Internet). The question is which *approach* is likely to help students become self-motivated. Answers A, B, and D relate to the particular situation. The only generic answer is C, which is the correct answer. Although the other answers might be good reasons to plan this lesson, **the question is** which *approach* is likely to help the students become self-motivated.

QUESTION 4.

Mr. Wong's class is confused about a social studies project relating to archaeology. They are confused about the steps in reporting their findings to the class. Several students have asked questions about the length of the written report. Mr. Wong could have best avoided this communication problem by changing his explanation of the project in which of the following ways?

A. Giving a more detailed explanation of the project the first time.

B. Being sure that all students are paying attention during the introduction to the project.

C. Handing out clearly written guidelines and discussing them as a class.

D. Providing students with a more detailed written handout.

In any question involving communication, the correct answer must include two-way discussions. A one-way explanation by the teacher (A) or written handout (D) does not allow for a clear exchange of information between teacher and students. Just because students appear to be paying attention does not mean they understand (B). Even though the written guidelines alone in the first part of answer C would not be correct, the class discussion included in the second part of the answer makes C the correct choice.

3

Indispensable Information

This information applies to all domains, so test-takers must have a firm grasp of this content before proceeding to the more specific information in the competencies.

GENERAL VOCABULARY

Vocabulary will be included throughout the study guide as basic information necessary for test-takers to understand the questions. Test-takers can test their knowledge of these terms and focus on unknown terms.

Advanced organizer: Structure providing a preview of the upcoming lesson.

Analogy: A logical comparison inferring that if two things are known to be alike in some ways, then they must be alike in other ways.

Collaborate (Collaboration): To work together.

Critical thinking: Evaluating information and logically solving problems.

Curriculum: What we teach.

Discourse: Verbal expression in speech or writing.

Domain: Related area.

Eclectic: Using a variety of sources.

Empower (Empowerment): To have control or be confident in one's own abilities.

Explicit: Clearly defined or direct.

Feedback: Information about the result of a performance.

Graphic organizer: Visual overview that shows the relationship of important concepts—for example, webbing or mapping.

Heterogeneous grouping: Grouping students with unlike characteristics or abilities.

Homogeneous grouping: Grouping students with like characteristics or abilities.

Implicit: Implied or suggested but not directly indicated.

Impulsivity: A tendency to respond quickly without thinking.

Instruction: How we teach the curriculum.

Internalize: To take in or absorb and make part of one's beliefs or attitudes.

Learner-Centered or Student-Centered: Teaching style focusing on the needs of the students.

Modality (Modalities): Preferred way(s) of learning such as seeing (visual), hearing (auditory), touching (tactile), or moving (kinesthetic).

Objectivity: Perceiving something without being influenced by personal opinions.

Paradigm: An example, pattern, or framework for thinking.

Pedagogy: The art, profession, or study of teaching.

Precocious: Advanced in development.

Proficiency: Correctly demonstrating a skill.

Project learning: An in-depth study in an area of interest done independently or in small groups.

Rationale: Reason behind a lesson or rule.

Reflection: To think back and carefully consider specifics of teaching and learning.

Rote learning: Memorizing facts or associations.

Scope: Amount covered by a given activity or subject.

Self-directed learning: The process of gradually shifting responsibility for learning to the students through activities that engage them in increasingly complex patterns of thought.

Student ownership: Taking control of the learning process.

Subjectivity: Based on personal opinions or feelings rather than on external facts or evidence.

Teacher-centered: Traditional teaching style in which teachers make all of the decisions focusing on the subject.

Technology: Any device used to complete an objective or task (not exclusively computers).

Terminology (terminologies): Vocabulary of technical terms used in a particular field.

Vicarious learning: Learning by watching someone else, without direct experience.

GENERAL VOCABULARY EXERCISE

After studying the General Vocabulary, test your recall by matching the word with the correct definition. Write the word in the blank by the correct definition. See answer key on page 107.

Advanced organizer	**Impulsivity**	**Rote learning**
Analogy	**Internalize**	**Self-directed learning**
Collaborate	**Modality**	**Student-centered**
Eclectic	**Objectivity**	**Subjectivity**
Empowerment	**Precocious**	**Teacher-centered**
Explicit	**Proficiency**	**Vicarious learning**
Graphic organizer	**Project learning**	
Implicit	**Reflection**	

1. _____ Gradually shifting responsibility for learning to the students

2. _____ An in-depth study in an area of interest

3. _____ Memorizing facts or associations

4. _____ Learning without direct experience

5. _____ Implied or suggested

6. _____ Advanced in development

7. _____ Using a variety of sources

8. _____ Clearly defined or direct

9. _____ Structure providing preview of lesson

10. _____ Preferred way of learning

11. _____ Visual overview showing relationships of concepts

12. _____ A logical comparison

13. _____ To be confident in one's abilities

14. _____ To take in or absorb

15. _____ To work together

16. _____ Thinking back and carefully considering

17. _____ Based on personal opinions rather that facts

18. _____ Tendency to respond quickly without thinking

19. _____ Perceiving something without personal opinion

20. _____ Correctly demonstrating a skill

Collaboration	**Heterogeneous**	**Scope**
Critical thinking	**Homogeneous**	**Student ownership**
Curriculum	**Instruction**	**Teacher-centered**
Discourse	**Learner-centered**	**Technology**
Domain	**Paradigm**	**Terminology**
Empowerment	**Pedagogy**	**Vicarious learning**
Feedback	**Rationale**	

21. _____ Related area

22. _____ The study of teaching

23. _____ What we teach

24. _____ How we teach

25. _____ A framework for thinking

26. _____ Amount covered

27. _____ Reason behind

28. _____ Evaluating information and solving problems

29. _____ Vocabulary of technical terms

30. _____ Grouping students with unlike characteristics

31. _____ Information about the result of a performance

32. _____ Verbal expression

33. _____ Teaching style focusing on the subject

34. _____ Grouping students with like characteristics

35. _____ Teaching style focusing on needs of students

36. _____ Taking control of the learning process

37. _____ Any device used to complete an objective or task

FLASHCARD EXERCISE

Flashcards are an effective way to learn new terminology. Use flashcards to **practice regularly** alone or with someone else. After completing the Vocabulary Exercise, make a flashcard for any word missed containing the term, the definition, and a cue for remembering the definition. Be creative in designing the cues and add any other information that might be helpful. Figure 3.1 shows examples of flashcards.

FIGURE 3.1 Flashcard examples.

Side one: **Side two:**

Paradigm	A set way of thinking about something **Pattern ForThinking**

Side one: **Side two:**

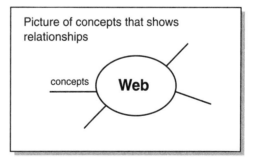

Graphic organizer	Picture of concepts that shows relationships concepts (**Web**)

RESEARCH-BASED PRACTICES

Test-takers should know and recognize the following practices identified by research studies as effective in the classroom. These are often included as correct answers on the Pedagogy and Professional Responsibilities (PPR) TExES.

Best Practices

- Utilizing **cooperative learning.**
- Promoting **critical thinking** and **problem solving.**
- Establishing a **learner-centered** environment.
- Creating a **positive** classroom environment.
- Encouraging **active** participation.
- Fostering **higher order** thinking/questioning.
- Fostering **school-home** relationships.
- Fostering **school-community** relationships.
- Celebrating **cultural diversity.**
- Maintaining good **classroom management/discipline.**
- Building on **prior knowledge.**
- Encouraging **risk taking.**
- Promoting **leadership** skills.
- Promoting **student ownership** of learning.
- Developing **motivation.**
- Encouraging independent/**creative** thinking.
- Making **real-world** connections.
- **Practicing** skills/strategies taught.
- Promoting **self-assessment**/evaluation.

Effective Teachers

- Utilize **heterogeneous grouping.**
- Utilize **discovery** and **cooperative learning.**
- Celebrate **diversity.**
- Utilize **reflective** teaching.
- Give students an opportunity for **reflection.**
- Foster **critical** thinking, **higher order** thinking and **problem-solving** skills.
- Foster a climate of respect, trust, and **appreciation for diversity.**
- **Evaluate** the effectiveness of instruction.
- Promote success and have **high expectations** for all (including special education/special needs students).
- Promote a **safe** and **orderly** environment.
- **Collaborate** with colleagues.
- Utilize **collaborative instruction.**

- Encourage **experimentation** and **risk taking.**
- Allow students to learn from their **mistakes.**
- **Maximize** learning/engagement time.
- View learning as a **lifetime pursuit.**
- **Plan** questions in advance.
- Follow the **chain of command.**

Effective Instruction

- Incorporates **real-world** contexts.
- Is learner/**student-centered.**
- Fosters **growth.**
- Is **multidisciplinary, interdisciplinary,** and **integrated.**
- Encourages **self-directed** thinking and learning.
- Includes a **variety** of instructional materials.
- Includes materials that are **developmentally appropriate.**
- Includes materials that are **relevant** to individual student needs.
- Includes **timely** feedback.
- **Validates** student ideas/concerns.
- **Connects** current skills to new skills.

Students Learn More

- When given an opportunity for **reflection** and **self-assessment.**
- When they have **control** over the learning experiences.
- When instruction is a **purposeful** pursuit based on prior knowledge.
- With an understanding of the **goals** and **objectives.**
- When they have a sense of **ownership** and self-expression.
- When they are independent, **self-directed** thinkers and learners.
- When they have been taught **metacognition** (thinking about and monitoring one's own thinking).
- When they are **accountable.**
- With **parental**/guardian involvement.

RESEARCH-BASED PRACTICES EXERCISE

Under each category of practices, put a check ✔ by recommended practices for TExES teachers and put an **X** by those not recommended. Answer keys for all exercises are in the back of the book. See answer key on page 107.

BEST PRACTICES

1. _____ Build on prior knowledge.

2. _____ Emphasize memorization.

3. _____ Utilize only teacher assessment.

4. _____ Use cooperative learning.

5. _____ Celebrate diversity.

6. _____ Teacher has sole responsibility for leading.

7. _____ Have a teacher-centered environment.

8. _____ Encourage risk taking.

9. _____ Make sure students don't make mistakes.

10. _____ Connect lessons to real world.

EFFECTIVE TEACHERS

11. _____ Collaborate with other teachers.

12. _____ Use homogeneous groups.

13. _____ Allow students to learn from their mistakes.

14. _____ Separate students with different backgrounds.

15. _____ Emphasize recall of content.

16. _____ Fit expectations to students' abilities.

17. _____ At the end of the day think back on the lessons taught.

18. _____ Think of questions as you go.

19. _____ Make the most of the learning time.

20. _____ Allow time for students to consider how they are learning.

EFFECTIVE INSTRUCTION

21. _____ Uses the same type of materials for consistency.

22. _____ Is learner-centered.

23. _____ Employs thematic units.

24. _____ Teaches new skills independently from previously learned skills.

25. _____ Is when teacher directs discussions by correcting student input.

STUDENTS LEARN MORE WHEN

26. _____ Teachers control all learning experiences.

27. _____ Teachers take instructional time to teach metacognition.

28. _____ Parents don't interfere with classroom activities.

29. _____ They understand lesson objectives.

30. _____ Instruction relates to their own background knowledge.

DOS AND DON'TS

The following is a list of good teaching practices used in TExES test questions. As stated in the test philosophy, practices listed under the **Dos** are effective. These answers will likely be **correct** answers on the test. Avoid selecting practices under the **Don'ts** on the test because they will likely be **incorrect** answers.

Dos	Don'ts
Active learning	**Passive** learning
Students taking active/major role	**Teachers** working/giving information
Concrete Materials to manipulate Hands-on activities Movement Communication/discussion	**Abstract** Ideas only Lecturing Paper and pencil Worksheets
Teacher-specified goals/objectives Using state standards or student goal setting	**Students** voting on topics/methods Using only textbook objectives
Cooperation/collaboration	**Competition**
Organized cooperative learning groups	**Unstructured** group work
Heterogeneous grouping Different ability levels Diverse proficiency levels	**Homogeneous grouping** Same ability level Same level of proficiency
High expectations for all students Consistent/same for all students Activities students can do **successfully**	**Flexible expectations by the teacher** Changed for different students Activities that **fail** students
Same goals/objectives for special needs students, bilingual, and English Language Learners (ELL) (as close to regular students as possible)	**Less** demanding, less effort, less work for special needs students, bilingual, and English Language Learners (ELL)
Emphasizing learning as a **process**	Focus only on the final **product**

DOS AND DON'TS EXERCISE

After studying the common teaching practices listed in the **Dos and Don'ts,** write either **Do** or **Don't** next to the following statements. See answer key on page 108.

1. _____ Homogeneous groups

2. _____ Teacher following specified goals and objectives

3. _____ Same expectations for all students

4. _____ Emphasis on final product

5. _____ Using hands-on activities

6. _____ Competitive games

7. _____ Activities designed for student success

8. _____ Students doing worksheets

9. _____ Different learning goals for special needs students

10. _____ Using only textbook objectives

11. _____ Students determining teaching method

12. _____ Using cooperative learning

13. _____ Grouping students of different ability levels together

14. _____ Lecturing

15. _____ Emphasizing writing process approach

16. _____ Students actively involved in learning

17. _____ ELL objectives as close to regular students as possible

18. _____ Tricky test questions that students are likely to fail

19. _____ Involving students in discussions

20. _____ Lower teacher expectations for bilingual students

WORD ASSOCIATIONS

When concepts (**in bold**) appear in a TExES question, the answer is usually associated with the words and phrases that follow.

First Step

Evaluate/Evaluation
Needs assessment
Assessment of background knowledge and skills through discussion
Self-reflection
Define goals and objectives
Investigate then report
Check local trends
Check with principal
Check with Site-Based Management Team (SBMT)
Prepare/preparation
Analyze/Analysis

Problem Solving

Open-ended   Inquiry/discovery
Relevance/real-world situations   Constructing knowledge

Cooperative Learning

Individual accountability   Group accountability
Social skills   Heterogeneous grouping
Interdependent rewards

Communication

Discussions
Must be two-way (give and receive information)

Technology

Motivational
Interactive learning
Internet = information exchange

Diversity

Celebrate   NOT pull-out programs
Heterogeneous grouping   Special needs
Including culture   Bilingual
Variety   English Language Learners (ELL)

WORD ASSOCIATION EXERCISE

After studying the TExES word associations, test your recall by matching the concept with the correct word or phrase. Write the letter of the concept in the blank by the correct association. See answer key on pge 108.

a. **First Step**   d. **Communication**
b. **Problem Solving**   e. **Technology**
c. **Cooperative Learning** f. **Diversity**

1. _____ Open-ended

2. _____ Discussions

3. _____ Needs assessment

4. _____ Social skills

5. _____ Motivational

6. _____ Two-way

7. _____ Celebrate

8. _____ Define goals and objectives

9. _____ Not pull-out programs

10. _____ Group accountability

11. _____ Constructing knowledge

12. _____ Self-reflection

13. _____ Including culture

14. _____ Inquiry/discovery

15. _____ Analyze

16. _____ Investigate then report

17. _____ Heterogeneous grouping

18. _____ Check with principal

19. _____ Individual accountability

20. _____ Interdependent rewards

COMMON VERBS

These verbs appear on the TExES test and often confuse test-takers. They are not necessarily content-specific verbs but are essential to understanding the questions and answers.

Adhere: To hold closely or firmly.
Advocate: To support or promote.
Affect: To change.
Celebrate: To honor or respect.
Detract: To take away from.
Diminish: To decrease.
Effect: To bring about (as change).
Employ: To use.
Encourage: To support or inspire.
Engage: To keep busy.
Enhance: To increase or make better.
Ensure: To make sure.
Facilitate: To make easier.
Focus: To concentrate.
Foster: To encourage.
Impart: To make known.
Implement: To carry out.
Model: To be or show an example of.
Monitor: To oversee.
Nurture: To help to grow.
Promote: To contribute to growth.
Pursue: To follow or to seek.
Reflect: To think back or consider seriously.
Respond: To act or answer.
Solicit: To ask for.
Stimulate: To increase or awaken.
Synthesize: To put things together to create something new.
Tailor: To adapt or modify.
Transfer: To pass on or get across.

COMMON VERB EXERCISE

After studying the common verbs, test your recall by writing the letter of the word next to the correct definition. See answer key on page 108.

a. **Effect**   f. **Promote**
b. **Foster**   g. **Encourage**
c. **Respond**   h. **Implement**
d. **Affect**   i. **Enhance**
e. **Model**   j. **Nurture**

1. _____ To act or answer

2. _____ To encourage

3. _____ To change

4. _____ To be or show an example of

5. _____ To help grow

6. _____ To increase or make better

7. _____ To carry out

8. _____ To bring about

k. **Transfer**   p. **Solicit**
l. **Reflect**   q. **Focus**
m. **Monitor**   r. **Synthesize**
n. **Engage**   s. **Advocate**
o. **Adhere**   t. **Facilitate**

9. _____ To oversee

10. _____ To put together

11. _____ To hold closely

12. _____ To concentrate

13. _____ To think back or consider seriously

14. _____ To ask for

15. _____ To make easier

16. _____ To support or promote

4

Domain I

DOMAIN I—Designing Instruction and Assessment to Promote Student Learning (approximately 31 percent of the test)

Standard Assessed

Pedagogy and Professional Responsibilities Standard I.

The teacher designs instruction appropriate for all students that reflects an understanding of relevant content and is based on continuous and appropriate assessment.

The content covered by the TExES exams is organized into areas called domains. Each domain covers a specific area of educator standards.

Within each domain, the content is broken down into a set of competencies. Domain I addresses the factors that teachers must understand in order to design effective instruction.

- Human growth and development (Competency 1)
- Diversity (Competency 2)
- Instruction based on goals and objectives (Competency 3)
- Learning theory and external factors that prevent learning (Competency 4)

VOCABULARY

Accommodation: Learning by changing existing knowledge structures.

Acculturation: Blending a native culture with a new culture, keeping elements of both.

Adolescence: A transitional period of physical and psychological development beginning around 11 to 13 years, extending through the teenage years.

Affective domain: Feelings, emotions, values, and attitudes.

Assimilation: Learning by adding new knowledge to existing knowledge.

Biracial or Multiracial: Having ancestors from two or more racial groups.

Cognitive domain: Memory, reasoning, and thinking abilities.

Constructivism: Learner-centered approach to teaching; students construct knowledge for themselves.

Cultural pluralism: A system in which many different cultural groups are valued and share power.

Culture: A way of life shared by members of a certain group, including values, beliefs, and attitudes.

Development: Changes taking place as one grows.

Developmentally appropriate or Age appropriate: Considering the age and stage of growth of the child in providing and planning learning experiences.

Diversity: Variety of different groups within the same setting.

Egocentric: Self-centeredness, especially in very young children.

Ethnic group or Ethnicity: A social group defined on the basis of its religious, national, or cultural characteristics.

Ethnocentrism: Believing one's culture is better than other cultures.

Field-dependent: Perceiving as a whole and preferring to learn with others.

Field-independent: Perceiving in parts and preferring to learn alone.

Guided practice: Practicing under the direction of the teacher.

Higher level thinking skills: The ability to use basic knowledge in analyzing, evaluating, or manipulating information.

Interdisciplinary unit: Many subject areas are included under one topic or theme (also called **Thematic** units or an **Integrated** approach).

Kinesthetic (Tactile) learners: Students who learn best by movement.

KWL: Stands for "What I **K**now, What I **W**ant to know, and What I **L**earned." Used as an instructional activity to establish student knowledge before and after introducing a lesson or unit.

Maturation or Development: The process of growing and changing.

Melting pot theory: The theory that cultures should blend into the main culture, losing unique characteristics.

Metacognition: Ability to monitor and think about one's own thinking, learning, and remembering.

Modeling: The teacher or student demonstrates processes, skills, or behaviors for learning.

Prejudice: Positive/negative mindset for a group of people.

Psychomotor domain: Physical activities or skills.

Salad bowl theory: The theory that cultures mix but retain uniqueness.

Scaffolding: Support for learning and problem solving that is withdrawn as competence improves.

Schema (Schemata): Mental structure(s) for organizing concepts and relationships.

Self-actualization: Reaching one's fullest potential.

Self-concept: One's perception of self (neither good nor bad).

Self-efficacy: Self-confidence that one can succeed (good).

Self-esteem: Feelings about oneself (can be good or bad).

Stereotype Assumption about certain types of people.

Tactile learners: Students who learn best by touch.

Zone of proximal development: Difference between what a student can do alone and with help from a peer or adult (Vygotsky).

VOCABULARY EXERCISE

After studying the Domain I vocabulary, test your recall by matching the word with the correct definition. Write the word in the blank by the correct definition. See answer key on page 108.

Accommodation	Psychomotor domain
Affective domain	Scaffolding
Assimilation	Schema
Cognitive domain	Self-actualization
Constructivism	Self-concept
Developmentally appropriate	Self-efficacy
Egocentric	Self-esteem
Maturation	Stereotyping
Metacognition	Tactile learners
Modeling	Zone of proximal development

1. _____ Self-centeredness

2. _____ Feelings about of oneself (can be good or bad)

3. _____ Memory and thinking ability

4. _____ Process of growing and changing

5. _____ Difference between what a student can do alone and with help

6. _____ Reaching one's fullest potential

7. _____ Students constructing knowledge for themselves

8. _____ Mental structure for organizing concepts

9. _____ Learning by touch

10. _____ Support for learning taken away as student progresses

11. _____ Learning by combining old material with new knowledge

12. _____ Self-confidence that one can succeed (good)

13. _____ Feelings, emotions, and attitudes

14. _____ Demonstration of skills to be learned

15. _____ Thinking about thinking

16. _____ Planning considering age and stage

17. _____ Physical activities or skills

18. _____ One's perception of self (neither good nor bad)

Accommodation

Acculturation

Adolescence

Assimilation

Cultural pluralism

Culture

Diversity

Ethnicity

Ethnocentrism

Field-dependent

Field-independent

Guided practice

Higher level thinking skills

Interdisciplinary unit

KWL

Maturation

Melting pot theory

Multiracial

Prejudice

Salad bowl theory

Schema

Stereotyping

19. _____ Many subject areas centered around one topic

20. _____ Assumptions about certain types of people

21. _____ Having ancestors from different racial groups

22. _____ Belief that cultures should blend into the main culture

23. _____ A way of life shared by members of a group

24. _____ Perceiving in parts

25. _____ Learning by adding new knowledge to existing

26. _____ Negative mindset for a group of people

27. _____ Social group defined by certain characteristics

28. _____ Students working under the direction of the teacher

29. _____ Keeping elements of both native culture and new culture

30. _____ Believing one's culture is better than others

31. _____ Analyzing, evaluating, or manipulating information

32. _____ Variety of different groups in the same setting

33. _____ Perceiving as a whole

34. _____ Valuing many different cultural groups

35. _____ An instructional activity used to establish background knowledge

36. _____ Theory of mixing cultures but retaining uniqueness

37. _____ A transitional period of physical and psychological development

Complete the Flashcard Exercise with terms missed from this Domain.

CONTENT

Competency 1–Human Growth and Development

BEST PRACTICES

▶ **Pay particular attention to matching the question with the answer here.**

▶ **Distracters are often valid developmental characteristics that do not directly apply to the question.**

- All instruction must be designed to be developmentally appropriate, focusing on what is important to each age group's level of development.
- Teachers must plan for short attention span and egocentrism at any age.
- Ability grouping negatively impacts achievement for all learners except gifted students. It also reinforces a negative self-image among low achievers.
- Early childhood students learn best through multisensory activities and discovery learning.
- Young children need manipulative materials and concrete experiences in the classroom.
- Adolescents prefer to construct knowledge on their own instead of passively receiving information.
- Adolescents benefit from interacting with peers during unfamiliar situations.
- The formation of identity is an important aspect of adolescent development.
- Early maturation for boys is an advantage, particularly athletically. Early-maturing boys are large for their age and better coordinated than late-maturing boys; therefore late-maturing boys suffer socially induced inferiority and are often treated as younger than their age by adults. They develop negative self-perceptions and are more likely to have conflicts with their parents.
- Early-maturing girls are likely to stand out in elementary school, have a precocious interest in boys, and have lower self-esteem than early-maturing boys. Early-maturing girls no longer feel self-conscious about their appearance in middle school. Girls are more likely to have nutritional deficiencies because they eat less and diet more.
- Puberty varies widely and affects how adolescents feel about themselves.

CHILD DEVELOPMENT

Child **development** includes the areas of **cognitive, physical, social,** and **emotional** growth. All areas of development exist simultaneously, and one does not exist independent of the rest. No one aspect of development is more important than another.

Cognitive—intellectual, mental, or thinking ability

Jean Piaget created categories for **cognitive** development in children from birth through adulthood. According to these categories, elementary students need concrete, hands-on (objects, not paper and pencil) activities through the early grades until approximately fourth grade. After that time, more abstract (in the head, hypothesizing, or on paper) activities are appropriate. Piaget emphasizes learning has to be done by the children themselves as they progress through the stages of cognitive development.

When children confront new or puzzling experiences, they must resolve inconsistencies in their understanding. According to Piaget, new knowledge is merely added to existing knowledge through the process of **assimilation.** On the other hand, existing knowledge structures change altogether when learning progresses through the process of **accommodation.**

Piaget's Stages of Cognitive Development

- **Sensorimotor (0–2):** Using senses and actions to understand the world; beginning to use imitation, memory, and thought; representing reality in the mind.
- **Preoperational (2–7):** Using representations rather than motor actions; ability to think through logically in one direction; thinking dominated by egocentrism.
- **Concrete Operations (7–11):** Logical problem solving only using hands-on materials; thinking in more than one direction (reversibility); understanding concepts of conservation and classification.
- **Formal Operations (11–adult):** Understanding highly abstract concepts; logical reasoning and scientific thinking; developing concerns about identity and social issues.

Lev Vygotsky provides a somewhat different view of **cognitive development,** emphasizing the importance of **social** interactions. Through **scaffolding,** the guidance of adults and peers advances children's learning through a **zone of proximal development (ZPD).** ZPD is the difference between mental tasks students can do alone and those for which they require help. **Assisted learning** or **guided participation** is a process the teacher might use when providing scaffolding within the student's zone of proximal development. This process helps students consistently progress in their learning. According to Vygotsky, children require other people to help them learn in a **social** setting.

Physical (Psychomotor)—development of the body

- **Cephalocaudal:** Physical development in a progression from head to toe—e.g., Infants can first control their heads, then shoulders, arms, and finally their legs and feet.

- **Proximodistal:** Physical development from the center of the body outward—e.g., An infant's head, chest, and trunk grow first, followed by arms, legs, then hands, and feet.

Social—emerging self-image and relating to other people

- Developing a sense of personal identity, answering the question "Who am I?"
- Socially competent means responsible, independent, self-controlled, cooperative, and purposeful behaviors.

Erik Erikson identified a series of **emotional** tasks people work through over the course of their lives. He discusses the emergence of **self,** the **search for identity,** and the individual's **relationships** with others throughout life. He defined eight **interdependent** stages through which people progress throughout life; the following six relate to the school years. Each stage is characterized by positive and negative emotions as well as a central emotional task.

Emotional (Psychosocial) Development (Erikson)

- **Trust versus mistrust (Birth to 12–18 months):** Forms a first loving relationship with caregiver or sense of hopelessness and uncertainty.
- **Autonomy versus shame/doubt (18 months–3 years):** Learns control and independence with physical skills or helplessness and embarrassment.
- **Initiative versus guilt (3–6 years):** Becomes increasingly competent and uses energy constructively but may be too forceful, leading to rejection by others.
- **Industry versus inferiority (6–12 years):** Explores new skills in a variety of areas and sets realistic goals or believes that best efforts are inadequate and unrealistic.
- **Identity versus role confusion (adolescence):** Makes deliberate choices and decisions or fails to integrate aspects and choices about people and ideas.
- **Intimacy versus isolation (young adulthood):** Willing to relate to other people and develops intimate relationships or overwhelmed and suffers feelings of loneliness.

Social Stages of Play Development

- Solitary: Alone.
- Onlooker: Just watching.
- Parallel: Next to another child, but not together.
- Associative: May be together, but no cooperation.
- Rough and tumble: Very active.

- Cooperative: Planning and working together with other children toward a common goal.

Physical (Psychomotor) Development

- Large muscles (gross motor skills) develop first; appropriate activities for young children include walking, running, jumping, and throwing a ball.
- Small muscles (fine motor skills) develop later for holding a pencil and using scissors; appropriate activities include manipulating clay, puzzles, and stringing beads.

Adolescent Development

- Resists adult authority.
- Will "try on" different roles and behaviors.
- Works on independent identity formation.
- Responds to real-world/authentic context and application.
- Is self-conscious of physical changes.
- Is sensitive to peer/social relationships.
- Has self-esteem issues.
- Begins ethical questioning.
- Has growing interest in broader world.
- Is ready to begin moving beyond school into adult world.
- Prefers to construct own knowledge.
- Engages in risk-taking.

Competency 2—Diversity

BEST PRACTICES

- Children from lower socioeconomic status (SES) backgrounds are less likely to respond to delayed reinforcement (more adapted to immediate gratification), less willing to compete, and more oriented toward cooperation with other children and individualized contact with the teacher.
- Children from lower SES backgrounds are less likely to achieve, are not as likely to be as well prepared, and are often at a disadvantage.
- Teachers should discuss ethnic issues openly, utilize cooperative learning, and avoid competitive games and ability grouping when racial tensions exist in the classroom.
- Students with special needs should be placed in the regular classroom.
- Teachers should first reflect on personal biases to try to eliminate them and utilize a variety of teaching methods that reflect a belief in success for all.
- Teachers should avoid grouping students by gender because it increases biases and stereotyping.

- Academically gifted students are often bored and need variety in instruction.

Diversity may include

- Race (skin color)
- Ethnicity (shared nationality groups)
- Gender (male/female)
- Culture (shared values, beliefs, and attitudes)
- Language (English Language Learners—ELL, English as a Second Language—ESL, or bilingual)
- Special needs
  - Academically challenged (low achievers)
  - Academically gifted (high achievers/creative ability)
  - Physical disability (wheelchair, walker, etc.)
  - Visually impaired (limited eyesight or blind)
  - Speech and hearing disabled
  - Other

Diversity should be celebrated, and the teacher should respond appropriately to diverse groups of learners. The teacher must model and encourage an appreciation for all students' cultural heritages, unique abilities, learning styles, interests, and needs. **Culturally relevant teaching** includes practices sensitive to the cultures and experiences of their students. The teacher should design learning experiences that include a variety of activities and resources from different cultures throughout the school year with **multicultural education.**

> **Multicultural education:** The process by which all students learn about similarities and differences and learn how to mutually adapt to each other.

Methods by Which Multicultural Education Is Implemented

- Interdisciplinary planning
- Unifying themes
- Learning holistically
- Materials from diverse writers
- Role playing
- Sharing cultures
- Music
- Interviewing each other
- High expectations for all
- Contacting parents

- Surveying parents
- Parents as guest speakers
- Keeping journals
- Discussion groups

The Educational Environment Should

- Empower students of all racial, ethnic, or cultural groups.
- Help all students function in society.
- Nurture positive interaction between students of all cultures.
- Draw upon and develop unique individual talents.
- Prepare all students to make contributions to society.

Common Misconceptions about Diverse Groups

(These would be **INCORRECT** answers or distracters on the test.)

- Gender
  - Males may tend to be overactive, or even hyperactive.
  - Females are expected to be submissive.
  - Females are not likely to be math/science/technology oriented.
- Asian Americans are smarter.
- Limited language students are slow learners.

Competency 3—Designing Instruction Based on Goals

BEST PRACTICES

- Teachers should perform a task analysis for each lesson to determine necessary prerequisite skills and appropriate level of difficulty.
- The primary purpose for planning a discussion is to facilitate higher order thinking.
- Research has established that group discussion in which students publicly commit themselves is effective in changing individuals' attitudes.
- The teacher must **FIRST** set instructional goals for the students' learning.

The state of Texas developed curriculum guidelines for all grade levels and subject areas called **Texas Essential Knowledge and Skills(TEKS).**

TEKS Do Contain

- Basic knowledge (not higher level thinking skills)
- Prerequisite knowledge necessary for attaining higher level thinking skills

TEKS Do NOT Include

- Activities
- Resources
- Assessments

The teacher must use the TEKS to plan the amount of time to spend and emphasis needed for instruction according to the needs of each class.

The TEKS must be covered by teachers at each grade level and are tested in the **Texas Assessment of Knowledge and Skills (TAKS)** test beginning in third grade. Students must pass an exit-level TAKS to graduate from high school. It is essential that teachers include TEKS in their curriculum because the state of Texas holds schools and teachers accountable for students' TAKS scores. This accountability and public attention creates a high-stakes testing environment.

Benjamin Bloom devised a hierarchy of thinking skills from lower levels, or basic skills, to higher levels that include more creative, problem-solving ability and critical thinking for students. When writing **objectives,** teachers should include higher levels, in addition to the prerequisite levels included in the TEKS.

Objective writing: Verbs used must be measurable to ensure students meet goals. DO NOT use verbs such as *learn, understand, know,* or *appreciate,* which are hard to assess.

Bloom's Three Domains for Objectives—Cognitive, Affective, and Psychomotor

- **Cognitive Domain:** Thinking, memory, and reasoning (divided into six levels), including appropriate verbs for objective writing at each level.
  - **Knowledge:** The ability to recall information presented earlier.

    state, define, identify, list, describe, recognize, label, recall
  - **Comprehension:** The ability to demonstrate understanding of information.

    explain, distinguish, summarize, illustrate, interpret, generalize
  - **Application:** The ability to apply information to new and old situations.

    apply, interpret, construct, show, solve, demonstrate
  - **Analysis** (higher order thinking:) The ability to separate complex information into parts and recognize the relationship between the parts.

    compare, contrast, analyze, infer, classify, categorize, distinguish

☐ **Synthesis** (higher order thinking:) The ability to gather information to form new levels of information.

create, develop, design, produce, plan, generate, predict, formulate

☐ **Evaluation** (higher order thinking:) The ability to make judgments based on given knowledge or standards.

evaluate, criticize, judge, justify, prioritize, appraise, debate, solve

- **Affective Domain:** Attitudes and feelings; must teach this through modeling.

Students will develop an appreciation of literature.

- **Psychomotor Domain:** Physical ability; must assess through student performance.

Students will be able to assemble the appropriate laboratory apparatus without referring to their notes.

A **unit** is the result of long-term planning. There are usually many **lesson plans** involved in a unit. Each lesson should fit into the goals of the unit of which it is a part. Unit plans should include:

- A title
- The overview (nature and scope, goals)
- Instructional outcomes
- Conceptual map (unit web)
- Timetable
- The approach (probable introduction)
- Activities
- Bibliography
- Materials
- Evaluation techniques

The **traditional lesson cycle** is one of the many types of classroom instruction and includes the following parts:

- Objectives/goals/TEKS
- Focus—introductory "hook" to get students' attention
- Connection to prior knowledge
- Materials
- Teacher modeling/direct instruction
- Guided practice
- Independent practice
- Assessment/Evaluation—check for mastery of objectives
- Enrichment/Extension activities

Homework is an extension of what is taught in the classroom. **Guidelines for homework include:**

- Set clear goals.
- Outline how it will be graded.
- Make students accountable.
- Determine due date.
- Do not use as punishment.
- Do not exempt or do away with homework as a reward.
- Teach students to proofread.
- For projects, have students turn in periodic drafts for feedback.

Competency 4—Engaging Instruction

BEST PRACTICES

▶ **Give particular attention to questions that deal with students' prior experiences, students' reflecting on experiences, and students' being responsible for their own learning.**

- Learning logs can be used to reflect on both metacognition (students monitoring their own thinking) and on the understanding of content being studied.
- Learning style is not an indicator of intelligence but rather of how a person learns. Teachers should identify learning styles of students as a basis for providing responsive instruction.
- Students need to have an adequate knowledge of a topic when beginning a discussion in which they will be expected to take a position and defend it.
- Prior learning experiences affect learning, so questionnaires or pretests are valuable in designing lesson activities.
- Teachers should encourage at-risk students to express themselves orally to provide opportunities for development of effective oral communication skills that are often lacking in their home environment.
- Because disengagement is problematic with at-risk students, the teacher must provide a confidence-building environment, including giving them sufficient wait time and expressing expectations clearly.
- Teachers often demand less from low achievers than from high achievers. Be careful to have the same high expectations for all students.
- Students pay closer attention and become more involved when the topics relate directly to their experiences and interests.
- Students prefer to construct their own knowledge instead of having the teacher give them the information.
- Teachers should teach to students' strengths, such as auditory, visual, or kinesthetic learning styles (modalities).

- Risk-taking behaviors should be viewed as a positive characteristic for learning.

Engaging Instruction

- Focuses on student needs/interests.
- Gives students choices or control over learning.
- Allows students to participate in planning to promote ownership.
- Develops student ownership in learning.
- Allows for self-expression.
- Builds confidence on small successes.
- Includes flexible grouping for a positive effect on students' self-esteem.
- Connects learning to real-world experiences.
- Integrates learning.
- Utilizes thematic, holistic, interdisciplinary approaches.

Teacher models reflection for students, in other words, the teacher thinks out loud. Teach students to reflect on their own learning—thinking about specifics relative to what they have learned. Students gain a sense of accomplishment through self-reflection.

Reflective Teaching

- Is a systematic process of reflection by the teacher.
- Allows teachers to assess their relationship with students and to make necessary modifications.
- Proves beneficial when reflecting on a lesson immediately before, during, or after it.
- Leads to continual self-monitoring and self regulation and allows teachers a chance to think critically about their teaching.
- Should bring about many questions to enhance effectiveness.

Metacognition Means Thinking about Thinking. Teach Students

- To be responsible for their own learning.
- To be independent, self-directed thinkers and learners.
- To own their learning.
- To be accountable.
- To **self-assess/self-monitor**
  - ☐ Think back.
  - ☐ List.
  - ☐ Evaluate progress.
  - ☐ Adjust behavior.

COGNITIVE LEARNING STYLES

Field-Dependent	*Field-Independent*
Perceives patterns as a whole	Analyzes patterns according to pieces
Has difficulty focusing on one aspect	Clusters and categorizes separate parts
Works well in groups	Prefers to work alone
Has global orientation	Has analytical orientation
Prefers teacher to organize learning	Likes own organization style
Is socially oriented	Is content oriented
Depends on others to set goals	Monitors own learning

Left Brain/Hemisphere	*Right Brain/Hemisphere*
Think analytically/logically	Thinks globally/holistically
Reasons inductively	Reasons deductively
Responds to verbal instruction	Responds to visual and kinesthetic instruction
Sees part to whole	Sees big picture
Remembers through language	Remembers through images/pictures
Processes step by step	Processes all at once
Is structured	Is creative
Performs well on structured assignments	Performs well on open-ended assignments
Reads for details and facts	Reads for main ideas and overviews
Thinks in linear fashion	Thinks with spatial patterns

Gardner's multiple intelligences theory states that students have strengths in certain areas. Some may not necessarily be "school smart." Students excel when given the opportunity to work in their own personal styles.

- Verbal-linguistic: Good with words.
- Logical-mathematical: Good with numbers.
- Visual-spatial: Good with pictures.
- Bodily-kinesthetic: Good with the body.
- Musical-rhythmic: Good with music.
- Interpersonal: Good with people.
- Intrapersonal: Works well alone.
- Naturalist: Learns through nature.

Effective Learning Sequence for Field Trips and Videos

- Use targeted learning—learn for a reason.
- Plan content to be logically sequenced within the curriculum.
- Use advanced organizers to provide a focus.
- Reflect on each part of experience to maximize learning.

Sequence for Processing New Information Through Higher
Level Thinking Skills

- Define basic information.
- Analyze observations by identifying possible reasons behind what was observed.
- Decide what you think.
- Evaluate importance.
- Defend choice.

CONTENT EXERCISE

The Competency Charts located in Appendix A will become your **"cheat sheets"** when studying for the TExES. Multiple exercises have been included in this study guide to help you internalize and retain the necessary information to pass the test. **You must commit to spending ample time studying these charts before taking the test.**

Cut out Competency Charts 1 through 4 in the Appendix A.

Highlighting Exercise

Understanding the language of the competencies is **CRITICAL** to mastering the TExES exam. **Exact phrases** and wording from the competencies may appear in the test questions and answers.

The **bold** words listed in the left column are in the test questions. The corresponding **bold** words in the right column appear in the correct answer and explain how the competencies should be implemented in the classroom. Highlighting the bold words in the left column then highlighting the corresponding bold words in the right column (while reading the entire phrase on right) will help test-takers identify **correct answers on the test.**

INSTRUCTIONS

Step 1.   With a **pink** marker, highlight and read the short phrase on the Competency 1 Chart next to the competency number. This phrase gives the **main idea** of the competency in a nutshell.

Step 2.   With an **orange** marker, highlight and read the sentence following the main idea. This sentence gives an **overview** of what you should understand about the competency and summarizes the bulleted phrases that follow.

Step 3.   With a **yellow** marker, highlight the first bold word in the left column of the Competency Chart. Continue across to the right column highlighting the same bold form of the word and reading the accompanying phrases. Go back and read the bulleted phrase in the left column in which the bold word is highlighted. Then reread for understanding the matching bold word form and phrase in the right column. The right column provides more detail necessary for understanding the competency. Making these **connections** will point to the right answers on the test.

Step 4. Go back and read any competency in the left column or phrase in the right column that was not previously highlighted.

Step 5. Reread the whole section of Domain I Content for Competency 1, highlighting in **blue** any **unfamiliar information** that you do not know and therefore will need to study before the test. Customize your cheat sheet by transferring in writing any notes to the Competency 1 Chart. In this way you will have one sheet of information containing all of the pertinent information for Competency 1. To be successful on the TExES you **must take ownership** of this cheat sheet by making it work for you. In the past, students have successfully used their cheat sheets to study before passing the exam.

Step 6. Repeat steps 1 through 5 for Competencies 2 through 4.

5

Domain II

**DOMAIN II—Creating a Positive, Productive Classroom Environment
(approximately 15% of the test)**

Standard Assessed

Pedagogy and Professional Responsibilities Standard II

The teacher creates a classroom environment of respect and rapport that
fosters a positive climate for learning, equity, and excellence.

Domain II addresses setting up a classroom climate conducive to learning.

- Positive physical and emotional environment (Competency 5)
- Classroom management and student behavior (Competency 6)

VOCABULARY

Alternative Education Program (AEP): A campus or district-level placement for disruptive students who have broken rules or laws.

Authoritarian: Requiring strict adherence to rules.

Classroom climate: Atmosphere or feeling from interactions within the classroom.

Classroom management: How a teacher sets up and runs a supportive classroom free from distractions and inappropriate behavior.

Conflict resolution: Strategies for settling disagreements.

Consequences: Results that logically or naturally follow an action.

Discipline: A system of positive guidance and redirection encouraging students to regulate their own behavior.

Learning center: An area in the classroom where students can work independently at their own ability levels.

Permissive: Allowing or tolerating leniency in relation to rules.

Prominent: Noticeable or conspicuous.

Sponge activity: A short lesson to involve students and to "soak" up time before instruction begins.

Transition: Moving from one activity or lesson part to another.

VOCABULARY EXERCISE

After studying the Domain II vocabulary, test your recall by matching the word with the correct definition. Write the word in the blank by the correct definition. See answer key on page 109.

Alternative Education Program (AEP)	**Eclectic**
Authoritarian	**Inclusion**
Classroom climate	**Learning center**
Classroom management	**Permissive**
Conflict resolution	**Prominent**
Consequences	**Sponge activity**
Discipline	**Transition**

1. _____ Noticeable or conspicuous place

2. _____ Atmosphere within the classroom

3. _____ Moving from one activity to another

4. _____ How a teacher runs a supportive classroom

5. _____ A short activity before instruction begins

6. _____ Lenient toward rules

7. _____ Placement for disruptive students

8. _____ Strategies for settling disagreements

9. _____ An area where students can work independently

10. _____ Results that logically or naturally follow from an action

11. _____ Requiring strict obedience to rules

12. _____ System of positive guidance to regulate student behavior

Complete the Flashcard Exercise with terms missed from this Domain.

CONTENT

Competency 5—Classroom Climate

BEST PRACTICES

- A student with unmet physiological needs (one who is hungry or feels ill) is less likely to have the energy to put into learning.
- Time-out removes the student from class activities and is likely to decrease interest.
- In a safe, nurturing classroom environment, students are encouraged to take risks.

CLASSROOM ENVIRONMENT

The classroom should nurture a sense of community and understanding in a climate of trust and respect. The classroom should:

- Be supportive.
- Be productive.
- Be responsive.
- Be safe and orderly.
- Maintain standards and routines.
- Help transition from one task to another.
- Encourage self-discipline and self-management.

Proper classroom management, monitoring, and intervention help to produce a positive classroom environment.

SELF-FULFILLING PROPHECY

If teachers have **high expectations** for their students, the students will achieve higher goals. If teachers do **not** expect much from their students, then the students will not do well. Even if students have certain problem areas, teachers should not have low expectations for their performance. This theory has been proved countless times in research. Teachers must maintain a philosophy of **dignity and respect** for **all** their students and set challenging but realistic goals for them.

MASLOW'S HIERARCHY OF NEEDS (SOCIAL/EMOTIONAL)

Maslow's hierarchy of needs range from lower level needs for survival and safety to higher level needs for self-understanding and intellectual achievement. **Higher needs can't be fulfilled until lower needs are met.**

Lower Level Needs Indicate a Deficiency.

Physiological—shelter, food and clothing
Safety—at home and school
Belonging—need to belong and to feel loved

Self-esteem—confidence and satisfaction in one's self
Optimum level for school success

Higher Level Needs Lead to Growth

Intellectual achievement—knowledge and understanding
Aesthetic appreciation—appreciation for culture, beauty, literature, and the arts
Self-actualization—fully realizing one's potential
Transcendence—development of intuitive abilities

Competency 6—Managing Student Behavior

BEST PRACTICES

- Reinforcing desirable behaviors (praising effectively, smiling at students who look attentive, cueing good behavior) motivates students to continue good behavior.
- A systematic reinforcement schedule for completed work is a natural reinforcer that is likely to motivate.
- Keeping frequently used supplies and materials readily accessible minimizes disturbances in the classroom.
- In dealing with any problem, the first step is to talk to the student to determine awareness of the problem. Then help the student to understand the significance of the problem before deriving a mutual solution.
- Varying the content of lessons and using a variety of materials and approaches can help prevent off-task behavior.
- A well-planned, interesting lesson decreases disruptive behavior and boredom.
- Peer-tutoring and cross-age tutoring are recommended ways of dealing with misbehaving students.
- Corporal punishment is a violent, dehumanizing, and ineffective means of discipline that goes against the purposes of our educational system.
- Classroom rules should be stated positively.
- Students should have a voice in establishing classroom rules.

CLASSROOM MANAGEMENT

Classroom management is a most important factor in teaching and is one of the areas that challenge teachers the most. There are **eight factors** of effective classroom management.

- Determining management style
- Determining motivational policies
- Establishing a positive classroom environment
- Establishing classroom rules and routines
- Using preventive techniques
- Understanding why students misbehave

- Understanding how to deal with serious behavioral problems
- Understanding the legal aspects of classroom management

A **positive classroom environment** is one in which learning is valued and encouraged, and students feel safe to take risks.

MANAGEMENT STYLE

Every teacher has a management style that demonstrates control in the classroom. Two types of control are **authority and power.** Classroom control goes along with the management style known as the **three Cs.**

- **Content**
- **Conduct**
- **Covenant**

When determining motivational policies to implement, teachers should consider that motivation ties directly to **content,** the first "C" of classroom control. Teachers should also determine what content they will be teaching and how to get students excited about it.

Once management and motivational styles have been determined, along with a positive classroom environment, a teacher is ready to establish rules and routines for **conduct.** Use a two-way discussion to encourage students to participate in making the rules so that they will be more receptive to obeying them. Keep the rules stated positively as a **covenant.**

Use the following four principles for planning classroom rules:

- Reasonable and necessary
- Meaningful and understandable
- Consistent with instructional goals and how people learn
- Consistent with school rules

Assertive Discipline

Canter's **assertive discipline** is a preventive classroom management approach. **Six principles** for preventive techniques to restrict discipline problems before they become serious include the following:

- Provide for students' needs in the instructional process.
- Encourage students to communicate what and how they would like to learn.
- Involve students in establishing clear rules and expectations.
- Allow students to help determine the role of the teacher.
- Foster the establishment of good relationships between students and teachers.
- Help students to learn how to evaluate their academic performance.

Reality Therapy

Glasser's **reality therapy** states that students will misbehave if needs are not met. An understanding of why minor misbehavior occurs helps with classroom disruptions. Glasser defined **four basic needs,** including:

- Love
- Control
- Freedom
- Fun

Teachers should help students meet their own needs in these areas.

Operant Conditioning

Skinner's **operant conditioning** suggests modifying behavioral problems by the use of consequences. Teachers focus on the observable behavior of their students and how behaviors can be strengthened, weakened, or eliminated. The **behavior modification theory** is based upon the notion that students' behaviors can be accompanied by consequences. These consequences have the ability to influence whether students will repeat such behaviors and if so, with how much intensity. The three types of consequences include:

- **Reinforcement:** Consequences given to increase or continue behaviors.
    - **Positive reinforcement**—something the student wants that is given
    - **Negative reinforcement**—something the student wants that is taken away
        (**Note:** Both positive and negative reinforcement increase behaviors.)
- **Punishment:** Used to weaken undesirable behaviors by using unpleasant consequences.
- **Extinction:** Removing reinforcers until the undesired behavior ceases.

DEALING WITH BEHAVIOR PROBLEMS

No teacher wants to experience dealing with **serious misbehavior** problems. A first step to addressing these is to research students' background and seek advice from appropriate adults. Using reality therapy and operant conditioning can help when a student is held accountable to a **contract.** Students agree with teachers to monitor and change their behaviors and sign a contract to that effect. It is important to for teachers to notice small improvements in these students and to positively reinforce them immediately.

The **self-discipline model** is superior to assertive discipline, submissive behavior, and authoritarian discipline because they are based on the premise that student behavior must be controlled by the teacher.

- Teachers should create an atmosphere that encourages students to develop control of their own behavior. In order to do this, students need to be convinced that it is in their best interest to conform to the teacher's and school's expectations.
- Instead of focusing on consequences for inappropriate behavior, teachers should concentrate on consistency, fairness, and mutual respect.
- A student's dignity must be preserved.

Classroom management must be consistent with the following:

- Policies of the school
- Legal system, both federal and state
- Students' rights

Rules must be publicized, rationale must be for educational purposes, and meanings should be clear with a compelling purpose.

CONFLICT RESOLUTION

Conflict resolution is defined as a method of resolving confrontational situations. The teacher's primary goal is to have students reach a mutually agreeable settlement.

Types of Conflict

- Beliefs
- Personal property
- Personal differences
- Territory
- Perceptions

Strategies to Resolve Conflict

- Diffuse with smile or humor
- Use positive words
- Seek additional information
- Involve other people
- Compromise or meet halfway
- Reach a cooperative settlement
- Encourage students to work it out on their own
- Separate upset students

Avoid

- Escalating the argument
- Threatening statements

- Placing blame
- Win–lose situations
- Owning the problem for the student

ROOM ARRANGEMENT

- Rows limit student participation.
- When in rows, students sitting near the front and center of the room are likely to speak more freely than students seated elsewhere.
- When in rows, students in the back of the row may lose interest.
- Room arrangement facilitates student interactions.
  - □ A U-shape facilitates student interaction during whole-group discussion.
  - □ Clusters of desks facilitate group activities.

CONTENT EXERCISE

The Competency Charts located in Appendix A will become your **cheat sheets** when studying for the TExES. Multiple exercises have been included in this study guide to help you internalize and retain the necessary information to pass the test. **You must commit to spending ample time studying these charts before taking the test.**

Cut out Competency Charts 5 and 6 in Appendix A.

Highlighting Exercise

Understanding the language of the competencies is **CRITICAL** to mastering the TExES exam. **Exact phrases** and wording from the competencies appear in the test questions and answers.

The **bold** words listed in the left column are in the test questions. The corresponding **bold** words in the right column appear in the correct answer and explain how the competencies should be implemented in the classroom. Highlighting the bold words in the left column then highlighting the corresponding bold words in the right column (while reading the entire phrase on right) will help test-takers identify **correct answers on the test.**

INSTRUCTIONS

Step 1.   With a **pink** marker, highlight and read the short phrase on the Competency 5 Chart next to the competency number. This phrase gives the **main idea** of the competency in a nutshell.

Step 2.   With an **orange** marker, highlight and read the sentence following the main idea. This sentence gives an **overview** of what you should understand about the competency and summarizes the bulleted phrases that follow.

Step 3. With a **yellow** marker, highlight the first bold word in the left column of the Competency Chart. Continue across to the right column highlighting the same bold form of the word and reading the accompanying phrases. Go back and read the bulleted phrase in the left column in which the bold word is highlighted. Then reread for understanding the matching bold word form and phrase in the right column. The right column provides more detail necessary for understanding the competency. Making these **connections** will point to the right answers on the test.

Step 4. Go back and read any competency in the left column or phrase in the right column that was not previously highlighted.

Step 5. Reread the whole section of Domain II Content for Competency 5, highlighting in **blue** any **unfamiliar information** that you do not know and therefore will need to study before the test. Customize your cheat sheet by transferring in writing any notes to the Competency 5 Chart. In this way you will have one sheet of information containing all of the pertinent information for Competency 5. To be successful on the TExES you **must take ownership** of this cheat sheet by making it work for you. In the past, students have successfully used their cheat sheets to study before passing the exam.

Step 6. Repeat steps 1 through 5 for Competency 6.

6

Domain III

DOMAIN III—Implementing Effective, Responsive Instruction and Assessment (approximately 31 percent of the test)

Standards Assessed

Pedagogy and Professional Responsibilities Standard I

The teacher designs instruction appropriate for all students that reflects an understanding of relevant content and is based on continuous and appropriate assessment.

Pedagogy and Professional Responsibilities Standard III

The teacher promotes student learning by providing responsive instruction that makes use of effective communication techniques, instructional strategies that actively engage students in the learning process, and timely, high-quality feedback.

Technology Applications Standards I through V

Standard I: All teachers use technology-related terms, concepts, data input strategies, and ethical practices to make informed decisions about current technologies and their applications.

Standard II: All teachers identify task requirements, apply search strategies, and use current technology to efficiently acquire, analyze, and evaluate a variety of electronic information.

Standard III: All teachers use task-appropriate tools to synthesize knowledge, create and modify solutions, and evaluate results in a way that supports the work of individuals and groups in problem-solving situations.

Standard IV: All teachers communicate information in different formats and for diverse audiences.

Standard V: All teachers know how to plan, organize, deliver, and evaluate instruction for all students that incorporates the effective use of current technology for teaching and integrating the Technology Applications Texas Essential Knowledge and Skills (TEKS) into the curriculum.

Domain III addresses classroom methodology and techniques for effective teaching.

- Communicating effectively (Competency 7)
- Active engagement (Competency 8)
- Effective use of technology (Competency 9)
- Assessment and evaluation (Competency 10)

VOCABULARY

Achievement: The amount a student has learned in a subject area.

Algorithm: A set of rules or procedures for performing a task.

Authentic assessment or Performance assessment: Demonstrating a skill or solving a problem in a real-life situation.

Deductive reasoning: Moving from a general rule or **De**cree to more specific **De**tails. (Example of this reasoning process: **De**cree: All insects have six legs. Specific **De**tails: An ant is an insect. Therefore, an ant must have six legs.)

Empathetic listening: Communicating understanding of students' feelings by putting yourself in their place.

Formative assessment: Measurement taking place both before and during instruction to guide lesson pace and planning.

Holistic evaluation: Judging the overall quality of project or paper.

Inductive reasoning: Moving from specific **In**formation to a general conclusion. (Example of this reasoning process: **In**stances: An ant, a bee, and a grasshopper are all insects with six legs. General Conclusion: Therefore, all insects have six legs.)

Inquiry or Discovery learning: Obtaining information by asking a question or investigating a problem.

Instructional strategy: Plan for how a lesson will be taught.

Mnemonic: A memory aid including tricks to aid in recall of information. (For example: **De**ductive reasoning = **De**cree to **De**tails)

Needs assessment: Discovering what is needed as a first step in determining a plan of action to address a problem or instructional goal.

Nonverbal cues: Physical acts that send a message.

Percentile score: Test score in comparison to other scores. For example, if a student scores in the 85th percentile, the student scored the same or better than 85 percent of other students taking the same test.

Pretest: A sample test given before content is presented to assess student knowledge of a topic.

Restating: To say again in another way.

Rubric: Set of scoring guidelines for evaluating student work to ensure consistency in grading.

Summative assessment: Measurement following instruction to **sum**marize students' learning and the teacher's instructional methods.

VOCABULARY EXERCISE

After studying the Domain III vocabulary, test your recall by matching the word with the correct definition. Write the word in the blank by the correct definition. See answer key on page 109.

Achievement	Needs assessment	Rubric
Algorithm	Percentile score	Summative assessment
Formative assessment	Performance assessment	
Holistic evaluation	Pretest	

1. _____ Judging the overall quality

2. _____ Amount a student has learned

3. _____ Measurement following instruction

4. _____ Set of scoring guidelines

5. _____ Demonstrating a skill

6. _____ The first step in determining a plan of action

7. _____ Test given before content is presented

8. _____ Measurement before and during instruction

9. _____ Test score in comparison to other scores

Algorithm	Holistic evaluation	Nonverbal cues
Deductive reasoning	Inductive reasoning	Restating
Discovery learning	Instructional strategy	
Empathetic listening	Mnemonic	

10. _____ A memory aid for recall of information

11. _____ Say again in another way

12. _____ A set of rules for performing a task

13. _____ Obtaining information by investigating a problem

14. _____ Physical acts that send a message

15. _____ Moving from a general rule to more specific details

16. _____ Understanding students' feelings

17. _____ Plan for how a lesson will be taught

18. _____ Moving from specific information to a general conclusion

Complete the Flashcard Exercise with terms missed from this Domain.

CONTENT

Competency 7—Communication

BEST PRACTICES

- Teachers should provide appropriate and nonthreatening opportunities for all students to be involved in the lesson.
- Praise serves to inform students what they are doing right; specific praise for right answers and appropriate behavior is best.
- Smaller groups are less threatening than whole class discussions, especially for shy students.
- It is more effective to call on students randomly so that all participate and are kept attentive during teaching.
- Avoid directing most questions at higher achieving students because lower achieving students will have a negative perception of their ability to answer correctly.
- Sufficient wait time (3 seconds) sends the message that the response is valued.
- A cultural norm against silence is the strongest factor against wait time.
- Divergent (open-ended) questions stimulate critical thinking and construction of knowledge.
- Always make communication two-way: teacher–student, student–student, teacher–parent, or teacher–teacher.

EFFECTIVE COMMUNICATION

Effective communication includes reflective listening and thoughtful questioning using the following techniques:

- **Prompting**—give a hint
- **Probing**—ask student to expand on his or her response
- **Verbal** and **nonverbal cues**—reminders or signals
- Discussion
- Modeling
- Guided practice
- Thoughtful questioning
- Simplifying
- Restating or rephrasing
- Specific meaningful praise

The teacher helps students see how past, present, and future learning is connected by using effective communication techniques to tie learning together into a meaningful whole.

Nonverbal Communication Cues and Techniques

- Eye contact—"the look"
- Hand expressions/Gestures
- Body language
- Facial expressions
- Proximity control—moving closer to off-task student
- Eye level—sit, bend, or kneel to look students in the eye to make them feel at ease.

Communication Techniques

- Persuasive—to convince others to agree with your point of view using strong feelings invoked through words or pictures
- Informative—to present information on a topic in an organized manner or a logical sequence
- Narrative—to tell a story through poetry, prose, art, music, or drama
- Expressive—to explain personal viewpoints using thoughts and feelings

Effective Discussions

- State the purpose of the discussion.
- Pose a question that stimulates and focuses the discussion.
- Define the rules of the discussion.
- Monitor and/or direct the discussion with key questions or redirecting.
- Probe in response to student input in order to keep the discussion going.
- Promote student to student interaction.
- Encourage listening skills.
- Summarize the discussion.

Effective Praise

- Be specific.
- Be sincere.
- Be spontaneous.
- Get students' attention.
- Choose words that are meaningful to the students.
- Don't overuse common expressions such as *good job, nice work,* or *right on.*

QUESTIONING TECHNIQUES

Effective Questioning

- Open-ended questions foster critical thinking and problem solving.
- Ask the question, pause, then call on students to answer (maximizes student engagement).

- **Wait time** increases the level of student responses because it gives students time to thoughtfully compose their answers
  - Wait time 1—time teacher waits after posing question before calling on student
  - Wait time 2—time teacher waits after student responds
- Types of questions
  - **Convergent**—requires one best answer
  - **Divergent**—many possible answers
- **Skilled questioning:** After posing a question, the student responds, then the teacher may use the following strategies:
  - Probing—getting more specific information from the student such as examples
  - Clarifying—restating the student response (helps students to reflect)
  - Redirecting—modifying a student response to focus the discussion in a more productive direction
- **Common questioning techniques to avoid. DO NOT:**
  - Ask all the questions.
  - Put words into students' mouths.
  - Show impatience with slow responses.
  - Ask questions with "yes/no" answers.
  - Assume that students know how to ask questions.
  - State the name of a student before asking a question.
  - Answer the questions yourself.
  - Appear to know all the answers.
  - Assume that everyone understands.
  - Call only on students who raise their hands.
  - Consider that each question has only one answer.
  - Plan to answer all questions.

Competency 8—Active Learning/Motivation

BEST PRACTICES

- Teachers should closely monitor student work and determine group size before assigning students to groups.
- Peer-tutoring influences students' social and intellectual development positively both for the tutors and tutees.
- Motivation is enhanced when students recognize the importance and value of the task.
- When presenting a new topic, activate existing knowledge or provide materials (books, charts, photos, videos) that will link new information to old.
- Engaging instruction is best accomplished in small groups.
- Engaging instruction is goal oriented and purposeful to focus students.

- Effective teachers stop their lesson sequence to capitalize on motivating events or activities that have captured students' attention (teachable moments) and connect to TEKS.
- When teachers use media such as videos or field trips, they should first specify objectives and discuss focus questions, then debrief students after the activity and hold them accountable for learning.

ABILITIES AND LEARNING ENVIRONMENTS
Accommodating a Wide Range of Abilities

- Feature topics that students have identified as interesting.
- Plan alternatives for high-ability students.
- Allow uninterested students to pursue different topics.
- Individualize instruction.
- Use peer tutoring.
- Employ hands-on learning in laboratory settings.

Ability Grouping (Homogeneous Grouping)

- Can reduce self-esteem of students.
- Often decreases achievement among average and low ability students.

Promoting Critical Thinking

- Teach for deeper understanding of content.
- Require students to justify the reasoning behind their conclusions.
- Help students develop metacognitive strategies.
- Inquiry, discovery, cooperative learning, and laboratory assignments are effective in developing critical thinking skills.

Three Types of Learning Environments

- **Competitive:** Use when specific skills are needed or to motivate students (**not recommended** due to possible negative effects on self-esteem).
- **Individualistic:** Use when time is important or teaching gifted or low-achieving students a special skill.
- **Cooperative:** Use when you want students to learn more and learn effective social skills.

MODELS OF INSTRUCTION

"A model of teaching is a description of a learning environment."[1]

[1]Bruce Joyce and Marsha Weil, *Models of Teaching*, 5th ed. (Boston: Allyn and Bacon, 1996), p. 11.

Models provide teachers with a series of steps to use in instructional planning. The teacher may use these steps as an outline, but need not follow them exactly in all situations.

Direct instruction: The teacher has the primary role in instructing the students.

Direct Instruction Models

Expository
1. Provide daily review.
2. State objectives.
3. Provide new content.
4. Allow for guided practice.
5. Provide feedback and correctives.
6. Provide independent practice.

Memory
1. State the objective.
2. Organize the content.
3. Order or categorize the content.
4. Link to the familiar (mnemonic devices).
5. Practice associations.

Mastery
1. Use cue set.
2. Provide best shot.
3. Provide guided practice with feedback and correctives.
4. Allow for independent practice.
5. Provide correctives and feedback.
6. Provide closure.

Lecture (older students only)
1. Begin with hook.
2. Use visual organizer on overhead.
3. Ask questions while lecturing.
4. Check students' notes for accuracy.
5. When visual organizer is complete, cover to see how much students recall.

Indirect instruction: Teacher and students share in the learning process.

Indirect Instruction Models

Concept Attainment
1. State objectives.
2. Define attributes of concept.
3. Provide positive and negative examples.
4. Test for attainment—feedback on examples and nonexamples.
5. Integrate the learning.

Discussion (Full class discussion of a topic)
1. State the purpose of the discussion.
2. Define the rules of the discussion.
3. Monitor and/or direct the discussion with key questions.
4. Summarize the discussion.

Reciprocal Teaching
1. State the objectives.
2. Define the process.
3. Make predictions about the content to be learned.
4. Read the content.

Directed Reading Thinking Activity
(DRTA) Reading new material
1. State the objectives.
2. Make predictions—record broadest possible speculation about content.

5. Provide for student-led
   questioning about content.
6. Provide for student-led
   summarization.
7. Clarify unclear points.
8. Repeat steps 3 through 7
   until content is covered.

3. Read.
4. Refine and extend.
5. Repeat steps 2 and 3.
6. Conclude.

Inquiry/Discovery

1. Present the problem, question,
   hypothesis.
2. Gather data and investigate
   situation.
3. Evaluate findings/interpret data.
4. Develop a theory or inference.
5. Predict.
6. Verify predictions.

Induction

1. Observe specific examples or
   data.
2. Describe common elements or
   features.
3. Discuss other examples noting
   commonalities.
4. State generalization.
5. Check it against new examples.

Deduction

1. State generalization.
2. Gather supporting examples
   or evidence.
3. Test generalization to determine
   if it is supported by evidence.
4. Revise or refine generalization.

Think, Pair, Share

1. Teacher poses a question.
2. Students think individually.
3. Each student discusses his or her
   answer with classmate.
4. Students share their answers with
   class.

Cooperative learning: Students work together to accomplish a shared goal
and take on the responsibility of one another's learning. Cooperative learning models such as those listed below are designed to include both academic and social skills instruction.

Cooperative Learning Instruction Models

*Student Teams–Achievement
Division (STAD)*

1. Present a new concept.
2. Form heterogeneous teams for
   study and practice.
3. Test students (individually) on
   newly learned materials.
4. Recognize winning teams.

Teams–Games Tournament (TGT)

1. Present a new concept.
2. Form heterogeneous teams and
   practice.
3. Participate in academic
   competition.
4. Recognize winning teams.

*Teams–Assisted Individualization
(TAI)*

1. Begin working on individualized
   materials.

Jigsaw

1. Assign heterogeneous teams
   to study topic.

2. Divide topic into parts and assign parts to individual team members.
3. Assemble expert groups to study the topic parts.
4. Experts teach their study teams.
5. Evaluate and provide team recognition.

2. Assign heterogeneous teams.
3. Have team members check individual work.
4. Student monitors give quizzes.
5. Provide team recognition.

Numbered Heads Together

1. Numbering: Teacher has students number off within groups of as 1, 2, 3, or 4.
2. Questioning: Teacher gives a directive to groups such as "Make sure everyone on your team can summarize the chapter."
3. Heads Together: Groups work together to master task.
4. Answering: Teacher calls a number (1, 2, 3, or 4) and only that student responds for each group.

COOPERATIVE LEARNING

Basic Elements of Cooperative Learning

- Positive interdependence
- Face-to-face interaction
- Individual accountability
- Interpersonal and small group skills

Benefits of Cooperative Learning

- Student–student interaction
- Accommodates a wide range of abilities, learning styles, and diverse backgrounds
- Improves self-esteem
- Encourages participation for slower students who are hesitant to become involved
- Provides opportunities for students to explain, rehearse responses, receive feedback in safe environment
- Improves achievement for all
- Exchange of ideas
- Develops social skills
- Adds variety

Teacher's Role in Cooperative Learning

- Clearly specifying objectives of lesson
- Deciding how students will be grouped
- Assigning students to groups
- Setting up positive room arrangement

- Planning the instructional materials
- Assigning roles
- Explaining academic task
- Structuring positive goals
- Structuring accountability
- Explaining criteria for success
- Specifying behaviors
- Establishing advanced group rules
- Monitoring student behavior
- Providing assistance during brief but focused interventions
- Intervening to teach collaboration
- Helping groups become more self-reflective
- Helping groups be aware of their own performance
- Providing for closure to the lesson
- Evaluating and processing
- Working with other teachers to plan

How to Teach Cooperative Learning

- Ensure that students see the need for the skill.
- Ensure that students understand what the skill is
- Set up practice situations.
- Ensure that students process their use of the skills.
- Ensure that students continue to practice skills.

Key Ingredients of Cooperative Learning

- Teaches academic skills as well as social skills
- Teaches group decision-making skills
- Teaches appreciation of differences
- Provider for peer assessment
- Uses heterogeneous grouping
- Allows higher achievers to deepen their own understanding
- Utilizes students strengths and weaknesses

Cooperative Learning Groups

- Effective cooperative learning lessons should be designed to ensure that each member of the group is accountable for his or her learning as well as for contributing to the success of the group.
- Cooperative learning lessons must have both **academic goals** and **social skill** goals.
- Use heterogeneous grouping (mixed abilities).
- Emphasize cooperation not competition.
- Increased noise is likely when cooperative learning is used, but research strongly supports positive outcomes with cooperative learning.

- Teachers must be trained to implement cooperative learning strategies.
- Gifted students often lack interpersonal skills and therefore benefit from cooperative learning.

Peer tutoring: Students instructing other students.

- Same age tutoring–Tutor is the same age as tutee.
- Cross age tutoring–Tutor is older than tutee.

MOTIVATION

Motivation: A drive to do something.

Types of Motivation

- **Extrinsic motivation:** Students are motivated by an outcome that is external or appears to be unrelated to the activity in which they are engaged.
  - **Examples:** grades, stickers, rewards, partial credit for correcting mistakes
- **Intrinsic motivation:** Students work because of their own desires, regardless of any rewards (preferred motivation style).
  - **Examples:** to fulfill personal goals, self-satisfaction, pleasure, enjoyment

Motivation Techniques

- Have high expectations for all.
- Relate content to student interests.
- Structure learning as a series of small successes.
- Build confidence through competence.
- Give students choice when applicable.
- Give students control over their learning when applicable.
- Give students a chance to express themselves.
- Use cooperative learning.
- Create a nonthreatening, warm, supportive classroom climate.
- Learn students' names.
- Use a variety of teaching strategies and activities.
- Keep students busy and active.
- Encourage slow and reluctant learners.
- Challenge students.
- Establish a climate of respect.
- Model desired behavior.
- Encourage parental involvement.

Competency 9—Technology

BEST PRACTICES

- Teachers must ensure **equity** in access to technology because some families do not have access to the Internet for information or communications, nor do they have access to a home computer for creating and developing projects.
- Technology typically increases motivation.
- Students must know how to evaluate web resources as a **first step** in utilizing the Internet.
- Using unlicensed software is illegal, and a teacher should remove all illegal copies of software from the computers.
- Technology should be utilized as a learning tool.
- Variety of media increases student understanding and effectiveness.
- Variety of media and technology encourages experimentation.
- Technology addresses strengths, styles, modalities, and interests.
- Demonstrate child safety software to reduce parent concern for Internet use and to incorporate various learning styles.

TECHNOLOGY TERMS

Acceptable Use Policy (AUP): School district's policy for use of school resources, especially school computers and the Internet; must be signed by students and parents.

Bookmark/Favorite: A time-saving Internet feature to keep an address or URL you wish to return to later.

Distance education: Linking students and teachers in different locations through technology to facilitate learning.

Hardware: The physical parts of the computer.

Hyperlink: An element in an electronic document or website that moves the viewer to another place in the same document or to an entirely different document or website.

Hypertext: Nonsequential text presentation.

Hypermedia: Special type of database program that combines text, graphics, sound, and video elements into a product with "clickable" links to present ideas and information.

Hyperstudio: Authoring system software originally designed for kids to produce hypermedia.

Input device: Translates information into a form that the computer can understand, i.e., keyboard, mouse, scanner, digital cameras.

Local Area Network (LAN): A network in which the computers that are connected are close to each other, many times within the same building or campus.

Linking: Navigating from one place to another in a nonlinear fashion through related topics.

Network Interface Card (NIC): Connects computers to a network or shared devices, applications, peripherals.

Output device: Translates processed information into a form that the we can understand, i.e., monitor, printer.

Search string: A phrase using AND, OR, NOT, or NEAR that narrows or broadens an Internet search.

Software: The programs that instruct the computer to do certain jobs.

Webcam: Camera that can be connected to the Internet for continuous images.

Wide Area Network (WAN): A network that extends over a long distance.

Teachers should model all three basic skills for computer users.

- **Technology literacy:** Skills required for competent use of technology.
- **Information literacy:** Knowing how to define, locate, use, and analyze information to accomplish a goal.
- **Visual literacy:** Interpreting the meaning of visual messages and using them to communicate.

SOFTWARE APPLICATION PROGRAMS

Application software allows the user to accomplish a specific task such as creating a document, worksheet, presentation, filing cabinet, etc. The following are examples of application software.

Browser: Short for Web browser, it is an application program that allows users to "browse," display, and navigate through the information on the World Wide Web. Browsers are capable of displaying both graphics and text. *Mosaic* was the first widely distributed browser, other common browsers include *Netscape Navigator, Internet Explorer, Opera, Mozilla,* and *Firefox.*

Computer Assisted Instruction (CAI): Instruction that utilizes a computer to present information to the student as a self-learning tool such as drill/practice and tutorial software.

Computer graphics: Software that produces all kinds of graphics, such as 3D animation, charts, and graphs; can be from the Internet, digital cameras, scanners, or from some software applications that include clipart within the program.

Database: Software that produces a collection of data organized according to some structure or purpose; can manipulate data in a large collection of files (the database), cross-referencing between files as needed.

Desktop publishing: Specialized software designed to combine text and graphics to produce high-quality output on a laser printer or typesetting machine.

Drill and practice: Software that provides repetitive practice on skills previously taught through teacher-led instruction or tutorial software.

Email: Electronic correspondence used as a motivational tool for practicing reading and writing skills through activities such as **E-Pals** or **Key Pals** (similar to penpals).

Groupware (also known as **collaborative** software): Software that allows two or more networked users to work on the same document at the same time.

Multimedia: Software that combines multiple types of media such as text, graphics, sounds, animations, and video into an integrated product.

Productivity tools: Software that increases classroom teacher's effectiveness; for example, grade book programs, puzzle makers, drill sheet generators, and test generators.

Simulation: Software that creates a lifelike but artificial environment with risks and complications removed.

Spreadsheet: Software based on the traditional accounting worksheet that has rows and columns that can be used to **present, analyze, and compile** data.

Tutorial: Instructional software that presents new information or skills in a series of steps that progress through levels of difficulty and understanding.

Word processing: Software designed to make the computer a useful electronic **writing** tool that edits, stores, and prints documents.

SOFTWARE PIRACY AND COPYRIGHT LAWS

Piracy occurs when someone illegally duplicates software that is copyrighted. An estimated $7.5 billion per year in revenue is lost to software piracy. **Don't do it** because it is illegal and also against the Teacher's Code of Ethics. According to copyright laws, with a single copy of a program you **may**

- Make one backup copy.
- Use a "locksmith" program to bypass the copy-prevention code on the original to make a backup copy.
- Install one copy of the program onto a computer.
- Adapt a computer program from one language to another if the program is not available in that language.
- Add features to make better use of the program.
- Adapt the program to meet local needs.

You **may not:**

- Make multiple copies.
- Make additional copies from a backup copy.

- Make copies to be sold, leased, loaned, transmitted, or given away.
- Sell a locally produced adaptation of the program.
- Make multiple copies of an adaptation even for use within a school or school district.
- Put a single copy onto a network without permission or site license.
- Make any use of the software documentation unless allowed by the program.
- Utilize graphics, music, or video without expressed written permission (for example, **Do not** use any Disney graphics or music clips.)

Competency 10—Assessment

BEST PRACTICES

- ▶ **Look closely at answers that concern student self-evaluation. These answers are likely to be the correct answers.**
- Classroom assessment should be learner centered; the goal is to improve learning.
- Tests should be closely aligned with learning goals and with what students have been taught.
- Feedback is most effective when it occurs immediately after testing.
- Grading based on improvement for a short period is likely to increase motivation and interest by making it possible for all students, regardless of ability, to succeed.

ASSESSMENT BASICS

Assessment vs. Evaluation

Assessment: Collection of information informing teachers about what students know.

Evaluation: Measurement or judgment placing value (grade) on student learning.

When evaluating students through testing, the test should be both valid and reliable.

Validity: The extent to which the test measures what it is supposed to measure.

Reliability: The extent to which the test results are consistent for an individual.

Assessment is generally either formative or summative depending on the use of the resulting information:

Formative: **Form**ing an opinion **along the way** about what the student has learned.

Summative: **sum**mary at the **end** of instruction; most often used for grading.

Pretests are used to

- Establish what students know.
- Identify misconceptions.
- Adapt instruction to individual needs.
- Help students assess their own knowledge.

Mastery refers to the achievement of objectives to a specified level. In mastery learning, assessment is aligned closely to objectives to ensure that most students will score high and master the content.

Knowledge of content can be measured by student work or student performance on assessments. These measurements indicate **instructional effectiveness.**

Types of assessments

- **Informal**
  - □ Teacher observation
  - □ Anecdotal notes/written records
  - □ Self-assessment—fosters a sense of ownership
  - □ Peer assessment
  - □ Informal inventories (reading, math, etc.)
  - □ Checklists
  - □ Journal writing
  - □ Portfolios
  - □ Play-based (for young children or special needs students)
- **Formal**
  - □ **Diagnostic test:** Identifies strengths and weaknesses.
  - □ **Standardized test:** Made by professionals to compare students on a broad scale.
    - • **Aptitude test**—predicts future performance
    - • **Achievement test**—measures levels of knowledge and skills acquired in an area
    - • **Norm-referenced test**—compares students to the average of a group of other students (norm group)
    - • **Criterion-referenced test**—assesses the level of mastery of a set of skills (criteria)
- **Performance Assessment (Authentic or Alternative)**

- **Observation:** Teachers watch and record students in normal classroom routines.
- **Constructed-response item:** Teachers ask a question and students respond.
- **Essay:** Teachers look for understanding in the written responses of students.
- **Oral:** Teachers listen for students' understanding and comprehension.
- **Projects:** Teachers review performances or presentations.
- **Experiments:** Teachers use a lab setting to assess student understanding.
- **Portfolio:** Students/teachers assemble a collection of work over a period of time.

TEST CONSTRUCTION

Types of test items

Objective: Good for factual information.

- True/false
- Multiple choice
- Matching
- Short answer/fill in blank

Subjective: Good for higher level skills.

- Essay
- Work samples
- Portfolios
- Projects/presentations

Guidelines for test construction

- Test main ideas instead of details.
- Choose questions that fit approach used in class; for example, use essay questions to test class discussions or multiple choice for more factual presentation of information.
- Use clear language and avoid tricky items.
- Give specific directions.
- Design objective items so that there is one and only one correct response.
- Design incorrect responses to represent common misconceptions for testing students' true knowledge and understanding.
- Be sure that objective items are stated in a parallel manner.
- Avoid statements that could be interpreted in different ways.
- Avoid copying directly from the book.

CONTENT EXERCISE

The Competency Charts located in Appendix A will become your **cheat sheets** when studying for the TExES. Multiple exercises have been included in this study guide to help you internalize and retain the necessary information to pass the test. **You must commit to spending ample time studying these charts before taking the test.**

Cut out Competency Charts 7 through 10 in Appendix A.

Highlighting Exercise

Understanding the language of the competencies is **CRITICAL** to mastering the TExES exam. **Exact phrases** and wording from the competencies appear in the test questions and answers.

The **bold** words listed in the left column are in the test questions. The corresponding **bold** words in the right column appear in the correct answer and explain how the competencies should be implemented in the classroom. Highlighting the bold words in the left column then highlighting the corresponding bold words in the right column (while reading the entire phrase on right) will help test-takers identify **correct answers on the test.**

INSTRUCTIONS

Step 1.   With a **pink** marker, highlight and read the short phrase on the Competency 7 Chart next to the competency number. This phrase gives the **main idea** of the competency in a nutshell.

Step 2.   With an **orange** marker, highlight and read the sentence following the main idea. This sentence gives an **overview** of what you should understand about the competency and summarizes the bulleted phrases that follow.

Step 3.   With a **yellow** marker, highlight the first bold word in the left column of the Competency Chart. Continue across to the right column highlighting the same bold form of the word and reading the accompanying phrases. Go back and read the bulleted phrase in the left column in which the bold word is highlighted. Then reread for understanding the matching bold word form and phrase in the right column. The right column provides more detail necessary for understanding the competency. Making these **connections** will point to the right answers on the test.

Step 4.   Go back and read any competency in the left column or phrase in the right column that was not previously highlighted.

Step 5.   Reread the whole section of Domain III Content for Competency 7, highlighting in **blue** any **unfamiliar information** that you do not know and therefore will need to study before the test. Customize your cheat sheet by transferring in writing any notes to the Competency 7 Chart. In this way you will have one sheet of information containing all of the pertinent information for Competency 7. To be successful on the TExES you **must take ownership** of this cheat sheet by making it work for you. In the past, students have successfully used their cheat sheets to study before passing the exam.

Step 6.   Repeat steps 1 through 5 for Competencies 8 through 10.

7

Domain IV

DOMAIN IV—Fulfilling Professional Roles and Responsibilities (approximately 23 percent of the test)

Standard Assessed

Pedagogy and Professional Responsibilities Standard IV

The teacher fulfills professional roles and responsibilities and adheres to legal and ethical requirements of the profession.

Domain IV addresses the job requirements related to the profession of teaching.

- Family involvement (Competency 11)
- Professional development (Competency 12)
- Laws and ethics (Competency 13)

VOCABULARY

Accountability: Holding teachers and schools responsible for student learning.

Administrators: Superintendent, principals, and other supervisors who carry out policies of the school board in a school district.

At-risk: Describes a student with a greater than usual chance of having difficulty in school due to factors such as limited English proficiency, cultural diversity, poverty, race, homelessness, or teen pregnancy.

Charter school: Experimental schools operating by contract or charter receiving public funds but following different rules than public schools.

Compensatory education: Special programs for at-risk students such as remedial instruction, special activities, or early learning experiences.

Compulsory education: School attendance required by law for every child, ages 6–19.

Confidentiality: Keeping certain information private only between people involved.

Ethics: Principles of good behavior, explaining how one should act in certain situations.

Inclusion: Including special needs students in regular classroom for all or part of the day.

Mentor: An established teacher given the job of advising a new teacher or a person who serves in a counseling role for a student.

Modification: Adjustment for students who are in need.

Novice: Someone who is new or inexperienced.

Professionalism: Conforming to the technical or ethical standards of a career.

Title I: Federally funded programs for students needing extra help.

VOCABULARY EXERCISE

After studying the Domain IV vocabulary, test your recall by matching the word with the correct definition. Write the word in the blank by the correct definition. See answer key on page 109.

Accountability	Ethics
Administrators	Inclusion
At-risk	Mentor
Charter school	Modifications
Compensatory education	Novice
Compulsory education	Summative
Confidentiality	Title I

1. _____ Keeping certain information private

2. _____ Holding teachers and schools responsible for learning

3. _____ Experimental schools operating by contract

4. _____ Adjustments for students who are in need

5. _____ School attendance law

6. _____ Special needs students in the regular classroom

7. _____ Superintendent, principal, or other supervisors

8. _____ Established teacher advising a new teacher

9. _____ Federally funded programs for students needing extra help

10. _____ Student with greater than usual chance of having difficulty

11. _____ Special programs for at-risk students

12. _____ Principles of good behavior

13. _____ Someone who is new or inexperienced

Complete the Flashcard Exercise with terms missed from this Domain.

CONTENT

Competency 11—Family Involvement

BEST PRACTICES

▶ **Look closely at answers that mention teacher–parent discussions. These answers are likely to be the correct answers because they indicate two-way communication.**

- To develop an effective partnership with families, teachers communicate expectations and goals for all students at an open house or in the initial meeting with the family to define teacher, student, and family roles for the school year.
- Begin and end a parent conference on a positive note, exercise self-control, and remain unemotional.
- Conveying correct information is the most effective technique for clearing up misunderstandings that may occur in a parent–teacher conference.
- Provide sufficient opportunity for parental input—involve the parent in the conversation.
- Pause and encourage the parent to respond and offer suggestions.
- Contact with parents should be ongoing, systematic, and positive rather than reactive to problems or emergencies.
- Teachers can be effective public relations agents by building a solid partnership with the parents.
- Parent conferences should be planned and scheduled in advance, giving the reason for the conference.
- The primary purpose of a parent conference should be **mutual** information sharing between parent and teacher—**NOT** a one-way communication either way.
- Concerning behavior problems, provide suggestions that will help the student rather than seeking punishment.
- Problems should be resolved collaboratively.
- Use all forms of communication with parents: phone calls, voice mail, regular mail, email, and notes home with student.
- If the home language is not English, notes must be sent in the home language.
- Serious problems or family needs may require the teacher to seek help from the school counselor.

Parent–Teacher Conferences

- Ask parent for convenient time for him or her to meet or talk on the phone.
- Begin and end on positive note.

- Don't use jargon or education terms such as *metacognition, TEKS,* or *TAKS.*
- Address parental concerns directly.
- Acknowledge concerns.
- Provide a translator if parents' first language is not English.
- Consider conference as partnering with parent to help student.
- Greet parents openly and warmly.
- Introduce yourself.
- Stay focused.
- Listen reflectively.
- Do not be defensive.
- Respect confidentiality.
- Avoid "labeling" students.
- Highlight student successes.
- Convey information correctly and objectively.
- Do not make judgmental comments.
- Do not compare student with peers or siblings.
- Suggest what parents can do to help with school-related problems.
- Never tell a parent how to raise his or her child.
- Arrange for follow-up.
- Be aware of cultural differences in families such as eye contact, personal space, and attitude toward authority.

Communication forum via the Internet using websites (school district's or individual teacher's) and/or email for parents and students to access information such as the following:

- Homework assignments
- Teacher expectations
- Instructions for projects
- Vocabulary lists
- Content to be covered on test
- Upcoming events
- Permission slips to be signed
- Student work
- Class newsletter
- Conferences when it is impossible to meet in person

Caution: Teachers must be aware that not all parents have access to this communication forum so alternative methods such as printed information may need to be sent home in some cases. It is the **teacher's responsibility** to find out **which families** have access to **electronic media.**

Competency 12—Professional Development

BEST PRACTICES

▶ **Look closely at answers that mention meetings with other professionals. Choose the answer that shows a two-way discussion. In other words, the teacher gives information and values the information shared.**

■ Teachers have not been effective in working cooperatively with peers because they are isolated from one another during most of the school day. Implementing instructional teams that meet regularly to collaborate and plan provides teachers with an opportunity to learn from each other.

■ Teachers should invite the principal to visit their classes to observe teaching methods and to build a positive relationship.

PROFESSIONAL DEVELOPMENT BASICS

Collaboration

■ **Vertical teaming:** Planning with teachers from other grade levels to eliminate curriculum gaps and/or overlaps.
■ **Horizontal teaming:** Planning with teachers from the same grade level or the same subject area to guarantee consistency within the district or school.
■ **Team teaching:** Two or more teachers planning and sharing materials and resources to deliver instruction more effectively.
■ **Mentoring:** Using experienced teachers to guide, advise, and help new teachers.
■ **Integration teaming:** Working with colleagues to develop interdisciplinary units of instruction.

School Community

■ School board
■ Superintendent
■ Curriculum coordinator
■ Technology coordinator
■ Family liaison/parent educator
■ Principal
■ Administrator
■ Specialist
■ Department chairperson
■ Special education personnel
■ Mentor
■ Colleagues

- Paraprofessionals/aides
- School/district committees

Site-Based Decision Making (SBDM): Teachers, parents, community members, administrators, and other staff work as a team (**Site-Based Management Team [SBMT]** or **Campus Improvement Team [CIT]**) at the school level to make decisions. This group is responsible for the **Campus Improvement Plan (CIP)** for school organization, curriculum, planning, budgeting, staffing, and staff development. (This team is not involved in day-to-day decision making or addressing complaints.)

Campus Improvement Plan (CIP) Elements

- Goals
- Timelines for achieving goals
- Measurement of progress toward goals
- Performance objectives
- Plans to achieve objectives
- Descriptions of staff and resources
- Student assessments and achievement
- Prevention and intervention plans against school violence
- Programs that involve parents in school activities

Evidence of Professionalism

- Enhancing professional skills/knowledge
- Integrating technology
- Working cooperatively with colleagues
- Acknowledging the importance of mentoring
- Using effective classroom management
- Making effective use of time
- Integrating curriculum across disciplines
- Accomplishing educational goals
- Having sense of mission
- Seeking information to motivate student interest
- Visiting other schools to collaborate with other teachers
- Networking with others in the field through professional organizations
- Reading professional journals for current research and trends
- Attending professional conferences and workshops

Professional Support Resources

- Universities
- Regional education service centers
- Professional organizations

- Inservice training
- Workshops
- Teacher conferences
- Online resources

Benefits of Community Support

- Understands school as part of a larger community
- Provides opportunity for interaction with community members
- Is mutually supportive/beneficial
- Establishes strong/positive ties
- Helps students cope with community problems
- Fosters student awareness of future opportunities
- Provides understanding of values/traditions of community

Professional Development Appraisal System (PDAS): This is the currently employed appraisal in the majority of Texas school districts. This appraisal system also includes the **Teacher Self-Report Form** encouraging teachers to do their own self-assessment by reflection. It includes the following eight evaluation areas or domains:

- Active successful student participation in the learning process
- Learner-centered instruction
- Evaluation and feedback on student progress
- Management of student discipline, instructional strategies, time, and materials
- Professional communication
- Professional development
- Compliance with policies, operating procedures, and requirements
- Improvement of academic performance of all students on campus

Continuing Professional Education (CPE): Teachers are responsible for continuing their education through participation in the following:

- University coursework
- Independent study
- Workshops
- Seminars
- Conferences
- Inservice
- Staff development
- Mentoring
- Curriculum development
- Other activities as required by the State Board of Education (**SBOE**) for certificate renewal

Mentoring: In Texas, every new teacher must have a mentor as a part of his or her professional development. Mentors are established teachers who observe and offer suggestions for improvement in teaching and classroom management. A productive observation should include the following sequence of events:

- Meeting to discuss the area of need
- Classroom observation and evaluation
- Meeting to debrief and discuss recommendations for improvement

Competency 13—Legal/Ethical Requirements

BEST PRACTICES

- In 1991, House Bill (HB) 2885 established site-based decision making that directed local school districts to move decision making from the central office to the school level (decentralization). For example, campuses practicing site-based decision making do not have to consult the school board or the superintendent when making decisions regarding student fundraising projects.
- Principle IV of the Texas Code of Ethics and Standard Practices for Texas Educators states, "The educator should not reveal confidential information concerning students unless disclosure serves professional services or is required by law."
- Teachers are required to report the progress of a special education student as often as he or she reports to parents of other students.

BASIC CONSIDERATIONS AND LEGAL PRINCIPLES

Individuals with Disabilities Education Act (IDEA): This law requires each school district to provide education to children at **no cost** to parents or guardians. **Six major principles:**

- **Zero reject: ALL** children with disabilities regardless of severity.
- Nondiscriminatory identification and evaluation: Nonbiased evaluation using multiple methods.
- **Free, Appropriate Public Education (FAPE):** For all children.
- **Least Restrictive Environment (LRE):** An appropriate setting in which all students may function to their fullest capabilities.
- Due process safeguards: To protect the rights of children with disabilities and their parents.
- Parent and student participation and shared decision making: Schools must collaborate with parents and students with disabilities to design an appropriate program **(Individual Education Program [IEP]).**

Admission Review and Dismissal (ARD)

- An ARD committee must include but is not limited to the student, the parents (or guardians) of the student, a translator, at least one regular education teacher, at least one special education teacher, a representative of the school who is qualified to provide or supervise the provision of special services (like the principal, counselor, or diagnostician), someone who can interpret evaluation results, and other individuals who may be of help in designing an **IEP.**
- By law, the **ARD** committee must place the student in a classroom with his or her peers, unless the student's disability is so severe that education in a regular classroom setting cannot be achieved satisfactorily **(Least Restrictive Environment [LRE].**
- **Only the ARD committee has the authority to change the placement of a special education student.**
- Parents have the right to five days written notice of ARD committee meetings, the right to bring an attorney to the meeting, the right to have an interpreter if the parent's primary language is other than English, and the right to audiotape-record the meeting as long as all attending are informed.
- By law, the ARD committee meets at least once a year to review, develop, and/or revise the child's **IEP.**

Individual Education Program (IEP): A legal document or contract between school district and family documenting long-and short-term goals for students. It includes

- Goals and objectives to be met
- Modifications to be made
- Least restrictive environment

Classroom IEP modifications include ways teachers must accommodate special education students, such as

- Allowing more time for tests
- Decreasing the number of multiple-choice items
- Decreasing the number of question items on a test
- Supplying highlighted reading materials

Teaching strategies for special needs students include the following:

- Cooperative learning: Disabled and nondisabled students work together.
- Peer tutoring: One student tutors another student.

- Multisensory approach: Using touch, hearing, sight, and movement.
- Study skills.
- Self-instruction training: Teacher writes down for student a method of problem solving.
- Accommodation: Making changes based on the needs of students.

Determining Placement

- This process differs from state to state but generally requires a referral to a committee that represents a local school board.
- Students are placed on a scale from severely deficient to extremely superior based on testing of capabilities.
- A referral for special education can be made only after every effort has been made to accommodate the student in a regular classroom.
- The burden of providing an appropriate environment should be shared by the special education and regular teachers.

Various Types of Disabilities/Special Needs

- Mental retardation
- Learning disabilities
- Emotionally disturbed
- Autism
- Attention Deficit Disorder (ADD) or Attention Deficit Hyperactivity Disorder (ADHD)
- Communication disorders (speech or language impairment)
- Physical disability
  - □ Visual (blindness)
  - □ Auditory (hearing)
  - □ Brain injury
  - □ Other health impaired

Family Educational Rights and Privacy Act (FERPA): The federal law that protects the privacy of parents/guardians and children. **If parents are divorced, both parents (noncustodial and primary caregivers) have the right to access student records.**

To comply with this law, teachers should **avoid** the following practices:

- Talking about children/families' personal information
- Having children grade each other's work
- Revealing to parents/students other children's grades
- Leaving grade records where others can see them

Section 504: Section 504 of Public Law (PL) 94-142 provides modifications for students who have a physical or mental impairment. Being a slow learner does not qualify a child for special education but could be addressed under Section 504. The students may be temporarily affected by drug abuse, illness, accidents, medications, or other conditions to qualify for Section 504.

The **home language survey** identifies children as speaking another language and is required for students new to the district. Parents must give permission for placement in bilingual or **English as a Second Language (ESL)** programs. The home language survey must be administered in English and Spanish or translated into the home language.

Bilingual education involves using more than one language for instruction.

Limited English Proficient (LEP) or English Language Learner (ELL) indicates that a student's primary language is not English.

Procedures for Administering State- and District-Mandated Assessments such as a TAKS Test

- Keep test materials secure.
- Use instructions given for administration or test is not valid.
- Follow test security measures—can lose teaching certificate.
- Follow guidelines in test instruction manual.
- Cannot change the wording given in the instruction manual.
- Cannot answer student questions about answers during test.
- Can answer student questions about test directions.
- Can give teacher-made or other practice tests.
- Can teach lessons about test objectives but not specific test material.

COPYRIGHT GUIDELINES

Copyright: For educational use a teacher may make a single copy of the following:

- A chapter from a book
- An article from a periodical or newspaper
- A short story, short essay, or short poem, regardless of whether from a collective work, an illustration from a book, periodical, or newspaper

The **amount of material** that may fairly be copied can be defined as:

- One illustration per book or periodical
- 250 words from a poem
- 10 percent of a prose work up to 1,000 words

Multiple copies cannot exceed the number of students in a class. There cannot be more than nine instances of multiple copying for one course during one class term, except for current news periodicals, newspapers, and current news sections of other periodicals.

Not more than **two excerpts** or one short poem, article, story, or essay may be copied from the same author, except for current news periodicals, newspapers, and current news sections of other periodicals.

Multiple copies must meet a "**spontaneity**" test and must preclude waiting for permission from the copyright holder, meaning the same spontaneity cannot occur the same time next term and the same materials cannot be used during the next term.

Concerning **market value,** copying must not substitute for purchasing the original or creating or replacing an anthology or compilation of works protected by copyright. It also prohibits copying consumable items such as workbooks and standardized tests.

Fair use is a copyright principle based on the belief that the public is entitled to freely use portions of copyrighted materials for purposes of criticism or commentary. For example, if you wish to criticize a journalist, you should have the freedom to quote a portion of the journalist's work without asking permission.

Fair use—exception to copyright laws: Four factors determining fair use:

- The purpose and character of your use (educational use is acceptable).
- The nature of the copyrighted work.
- The amount and substantiality of the portion taken.
- The effect of the use upon the potential market.

CODE OF ETHICS

Code of Ethics for Teachers in Texas: Developed by SBEC as standard practices for Texas educators.

- School equipment (computers, tape recorders, cameras, etc.) can only be used outside of the school for school business.
- Teachers should not exclude, deny benefits, or grant advantage on the basis of:
  - Race
  - Color
  - Gender
  - Disability
  - National origin
  - Religion
  - Family status
- Teachers should not knowingly treat students in a way that negatively affects:
  - Student learning
  - Physical health
  - Mental health
  - Safety

- Teachers may not share confidential information or gossip about students and their families.
- Teachers may share information regarding students as long as the students cannot be identified.

Code of Ethics and Standard Practices for Texas Educators

STATEMENT OF PURPOSE

The Texas educator shall comply with standard practices and ethical conduct toward students, professional colleagues, school officials, parents, and members of the community and shall safeguard academic freedom. The Texas educator, in maintaining the dignity of the profession, shall **respect and obey the law,** demonstrate personal integrity, and exemplify honesty. The Texas educator, in exemplifying ethical relations with colleagues, shall extend just and equitable treatment to all members of the profession. The Texas educator, in accepting a position of public trust, shall measure success by the progress of each student toward realization of his or her potential as an effective citizen. The Texas educator, in fulfilling responsibilities in the community, shall cooperate with parents and others to improve the public schools of the community.

ENFORCEABLE STANDARDS

I. Professional Ethical Conduct, Practices and Performance.

Standard 1.1.   The educator shall not knowingly engage in **deceptive practices** regarding official policies of the school district or educational institution.

Standard 1.2.   The educator shall not knowingly **misappropriate,** divert, or use monies, personnel, property, or equipment committed to his or her charge for personal gain or advantage.

Standard 1.3.   The educator shall not submit **fraudulent** requests for reimbursement, expenses, or pay.

Standard 1.4.   The educator shall not use institutional or professional **privileges** for personal or partisan advantage.

Standard 1.5.   The educator shall neither accept nor offer **gratuities, gifts, or favors** that impair professional judgment or to obtain special advantage. This standard shall not restrict the acceptance of gifts or tokens offered and accepted openly from students, parents, or other persons or organizations in recognition or appreciation of service.

Standard 1.6.   The educator shall not **falsify records** or direct or coerce others to do so.

Standard 1.7.   The educator shall comply with state regulations, written local school board policies, and other applicable state and federal **laws.**

Standard 1.8.   The educator shall apply for, accept, offer, or assign a position or a responsibility on the basis of **professional qualifications.**

II. *Ethical Conduct Toward Professional Colleagues.*

Standard 2.1.   The educator shall not reveal **confidential** health or personnel information concerning colleagues unless disclosure serves lawful professional purposes or is required by law.

Standard 2.2.   The educator shall not harm others by knowingly making **false statements** about a colleague or the school system.

Standard 2.3.   The educator shall adhere to written local school board policies and state and federal laws regarding the **hiring, evaluation, and dismissal** of personnel.

Standard 2.4.   The educator shall not interfere with a colleague's exercise of political, professional, or citizenship **rights and responsibilities.**

Standard 2.5.   The educator shall not **discriminate** against or coerce a colleague on the basis of race, color, religion, national origin, age, sex, disability, or family status.

Standard 2.6.   The educator shall not use **coercive** means or promise of special treatment in order to influence professional decisions or colleagues.

Standard 2.7   The educator shall not **retaliate** against any individual who has filed a complaint with the SBEC under this chapter.

III. *Ethical Conduct Toward Students.*

Standard 3.1.   The educator shall not reveal **confidential** information concerning students unless disclosure serves lawful professional purposes or is required by law.

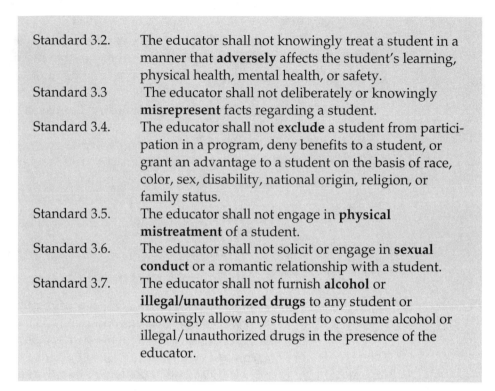

Standard 3.2.	The educator shall not knowingly treat a student in a manner that **adversely** affects the student's learning, physical health, mental health, or safety.
Standard 3.3	The educator shall not deliberately or knowingly **misrepresent** facts regarding a student.
Standard 3.4.	The educator shall not **exclude** a student from participation in a program, deny benefits to a student, or grant an advantage to a student on the basis of race, color, sex, disability, national origin, religion, or family status.
Standard 3.5.	The educator shall not engage in **physical mistreatment** of a student.
Standard 3.6.	The educator shall not solicit or engage in **sexual conduct** or a romantic relationship with a student.
Standard 3.7.	The educator shall not furnish **alcohol** or **illegal/unauthorized drugs** to any student or knowingly allow any student to consume alcohol or illegal/unauthorized drugs in the presence of the educator.

CONTENT EXERCISE

The Competency Charts located in Appendix A will become your **"cheat sheets"** when studying for the TExES. Multiple exercises have been included in this study guide to help you internalize and retain the necessary information to pass the test. **You must commit to spending ample time studying these charts before taking the test.**

Cut out Competency Charts 11 through 13 in Appendix A.

Highlighting Exercise

Understanding the language of the competencies is **CRITICAL** to mastering the TExES exam. **Exact phrases** and wording from the competencies appear in the test questions and answers.

The **bold** words listed in the left column are in the test questions. The corresponding **bold** words in the right column appear in the correct answer and explain how the competencies should be implemented in the classroom. Highlighting the bold words in the left column then highlighting the corresponding bold words in the right column (while reading the entire phrase on right) will help test-takers identify **correct answers on the test.**

INSTRUCTIONS

Step 1. With a **pink** marker, highlight and read the short phrase on the Competency 11 Chart next to the competency number. This phrase gives the **main idea** of the competency in a nutshell.

Step 2. With an **orange** marker, highlight and read the sentence following the main idea. This sentence gives an **overview** of what you should understand about the competency and summarizes the bulleted phrases that follow.

Step 3. With a **yellow** marker, highlight the first bold word in the left column of the Competency Chart. Continue across to the right column highlighting the same bold form of the word and reading the accompanying phrases. Go back and read the bulleted phrase in the left column in which the bold word is highlighted. Then reread for understanding the matching bold word form and phrase in the right column. The right column provides more detail necessary for understanding the competency. Making these **connections** will point to the right answers on the test.

Step 4. Go back and read any competency in the left column or phrase in the right column that was not previously highlighted.

Step 5. Reread the whole section of Domain IV Content for Competency 11, highlighting in **blue** any **unfamiliar information** that you do not know and therefore will need to study before the test.

Customize your cheat sheet by transferring in writing any notes to the Competency 11 Chart. In this way you will have one sheet of information containing all of the pertinent information for Competency 11. To be successful on the TExES you **must take ownership** of this cheat sheet by making it work for you. In the past, students have successfully used their cheat sheets to study before passing the exam.

Step 6.   Repeat steps 1 through 5 for Competencies 12 and 13.

8

Final Exercises

ABBREVIATIONS EXERCISE

Many terms used in education are often abbreviated. These abbreviations often show up on the PPR test questions. Go back through this study guide to collect and list unfamiliar abbreviations and what they mean in Table 8.1.

TABLE 8.1   Abbreviations Exercise

For example: IEP–Individual Education Program	

PRACTICE TEST ANALYSIS EXERCISE

Before completing these final exercises, go to the TExES website http://www.texes.ets.org and click on the link called **Preparation Materials.** Look under Preparation Manuals. Find and print the PPR study guide for your area of certification. Take the practice test provided utilizing the question dissection process. **This exercise helps you to quickly recognize what correct answers on the test will look like for each competency.**

Cut out the Practice Test Analysis Charts located in Appendix B to use in analyzing the practice test from the TExES Preparation Manual. For each of the thirteen competencies:

- Write the main idea of the competency under the number.
- Locate all questions on practice test for the competency and write the numbers in the first column.
- For each question, **summarize** what the question is asking in the second column.
- For each question, **summarize** the correct answer in the third column.
- After completing all questions for one competency, study all correct answer summaries and determine any associations that might help you remember what correct answers should look like. Write your word associations in the blank at the top right of the chart under "Keyword Phrases."
- Summaries and Keyword Phrases will help you identify correct answers on the test.

SYNTHESIS EXERCISE

The purpose of this final exercise is to synthesize your knowledge and skills for success on the TExES. You have studied each competency individually as well as general test-taking strategies. To bring it all together, go back to Chapter 2, Indispensable Information, and each competency in the study guide. Review the vocabulary, content, and competency charts for each. Determine what possible correct and incorrect answers might look like for each category and list in Table 8.2.

TABLE 8.2 Synthesis Exercise

Correct Answer Possibilities Indispensable Information:	Incorrect Answer Possibilities
For Example: Utilizing real-world connections for lessons like grocery shopping for a math lesson (from Research-Based Practices) Consistent expectations for all students including special needs and ELL (from Dos and Don'ts)	Using repetitive practice on math problems from the textbook Lowered expectations for bilingual students
Competency 1	

Competency 2	
Competency 3	
Competency 4	
Competency 5	

Competency 6	
Competency 7	
Competency 8	
Competency 9	

Competency 10	
Competency 11	
Competency 12	
Competency 13	

Exercise Answer Keys

GENERAL VOCABULARY EXERCISE (pp. 17–18)

1. Self-directed learning
2. Project learning
3. Rote learning
4. Vicarious learning
5. Implicit
6. Precocious
7. Eclectic
8. Explicit
9. Advanced organizer
10. Modality
11. Graphic organizer
12. Analogy
13. Empowerment
14. Internalize
15. Collaborate
16. Reflection
17. Subjectivity
18. Impulsivity
19. Objectivity
20. Proficiency
21. Domain
22. Pedagogy
23. Curriculum
24. Instruction
25. Paradigm
26. Scope
27. Rationale
28. Critical thinking
29. Terminology
30. Heterogeneous
31. Feedback
32. Discourse
33. Teacher-centered
34. Homogeneous
35. Learner-centered
36. Student ownership
37. Technology

RESEARCH-BASED PRACTICES EXERCISE (pp. 22–23)

1. ✔
2. ✗
3. ✗
4. ✔
5. ✔
6. ✗
7. ✗
8. ✔
9. ✗
10. ✔
11. ✔
12. ✗
13. ✔
14. ✗
15. ✗
16. ✗
17. ✔
18. ✗
19. ✔
20. ✔
21. ✗
22. ✔
23. ✔
24. ✗
25. ✗
26. ✗
27. ✔
28. ✗
29. ✔
30. ✔

DOS AND DON'TS EXERCISE (p. 25)

1. Don't	8. Don't	15. Do
2. Do	9. Don't	16. Do
3. Do	10. Don't	17. Do
4. Don't	11. Don't	18. Don't
5. Do	12. Do	19. Do
6. Don't	13. Do	20. Don't
7. Do	14. Don't	

WORD ASSOCIATION EXERCISE (p. 27)

1. b	8. a	15. a
2. d	9. f	16. a
3. a	10. c	17. c or f
4. c	11. b	18. a
5. e	12. a	19. c
6. d	13. f	20. c
7. f	14. b	

COMMON VERB EXERCISE (p. 29)

1. c	7. h	13. l
2. b	8. a	14. p
3. d	9. m	15. t
4. e	10. r	16. s
5. j	11. o	
6. i	12. q	

VOCABULARY EXERCISES

Domain I (pp. 34–35)

1. Egocentrism	14. Modeling	27. Ethnicity
2. Self-esteem	15. Metacognition	28. Guided practice
3. Cognitive domain	16. Developmentally	29. Acculturation
4. Maturation	appropriate	30. Ethnocentrism
5. Zone of proximal	17. Psychomotor domain	31. Higher level thinking
development	18. Self-concept	skills
6. Self-actualization	19. Interdisciplinary unit	32. Diversity
7. Constructivism	20. Stereotyping	33. Field-dependent
8. Schema	21. Multiracial	34. Cultural pluralism
9. Tactile	22. Melting pot theory	35. KWL
10. Scaffolding	23. Culture	36. Salad bowl theory
11. Accommodation	24. Field-independent	37. Adolescence
12. Self-efficacy	25. Assimilation	
13. Affective domain	26. Prejudice	

Domain II (p. 51)

1. Prominent
2. Classroom climate
3. Transition
4. Classroom management
5. Sponge activity

6. Permissive
7. Alternative Education Program
8. Conflict resolution
9. Learning center

10. Consequences
11. Authoritarian
12. Discipline

Domain III (p. 62)

1. Holistic evaluation
2. Achievement
3. Summative assessment
4. Rubric
5. Performance assessment
6. Needs assessment

7. Pretest
8. Formative assessment
9. Percentile score
10. Mnemonic
11. Restating
12. Algorithm

13. Discovery learning
14. Nonverbal cues
15. Deductive reasoning
16. Empathetic listening
17. Instructional strategy
18. Inductive reasoning

Domain IV (p. 83)

1. Confidentiality
2. Accountability
3. Charter school
4. Modifications
5. Compulsory education

6. Inclusion
7. Administrators
8. Mentors
9. Title I
10. At-risk

11. Compensatory education
12. Ethics
13. Novice

APPENDIX

Competency Charts

When studying for the TExES exam, these charts should be your "cheat sheets" for each competency. You should write any information you are trying to remember about a competency on that chart.

The left column contains phrases from the test question stems, and the right column contains correct answers.

It is critical to associate the wording of the competencies on the left with the correct answers on the right. Review these charts immediately before taking the test.

Cut along dotted line

112

COMPETENCY 1–Human Growth and Development

The teacher understands human developmental processes and applies this knowledge to plan instruction and ongoing assessment that motivate students and are responsive to their developmental characteristics and needs.

The beginning teacher:

- Knows the typical **stages of cognitive, social,** physical, and **emotional** development of students in early childhood through 12.

- Recognizes the wide range of individual **developmental** differences that characterizes students in early childhood through grade 12 and the implications of this developmental variation for instructional planning.

- Analyzes ways in which **developmental** characteristics of students in early childhood through grade 12 impact learning and performance; and applies knowledge of students' developmental characteristics and needs to plan effective learning experiences and assessments.

- Demonstrates an understanding of physical changes that occur in early childhood through adolescence, factors that influence students' physical growth and health (e.g., nutrition, sleep, prenatal exposure to drugs, abuse), and ways in which physical development impacts development in other domains (i.e., **cognitive, social, emotional**).

- Recognizes factors affecting the **social** and **emotional** development of students in early childhood through adolescence (e.g., lack of affection and attention, parental divorce, homelessness), and knows that students' social and emotional development impacts their development in other domains (i.e., **cognitive,** physical).

- Uses knowledge of cognitive changes in students in early childhood through adolescence (e.g., from an emphasis on concrete thinking to the emergence and refinement of abstract thinking and reasoning, reflective thinking, increased focus on the world beyond the school setting) to plan **developmentally appropriate** instruction and assessment that promote learning and development.

- Understands that development in any one **domain** (i.e., **cognitive, social, physical, emotional**) impacts development in other domains.

- Recognizes signs of **developmental delays** or impairments in students in early childhood through grade 4.

- Knows the **stages of play** development (i.e., from solitary to cooperative) and the important role of play in young children's learning and development.

- Uses knowledge of the developmental characteristics and needs of students in early childhood through grade 4 to plan meaningful, **integrated,** and active learning and **play** experiences that promote the development of the whole child.

Know that social life is important—distractions are many.

Foster **social** and **emotional** maturity and growth.

Piaget's **Cognitive Development stages:**
- Sensorimotor birth-2
- Preoperational 2-7
- Operational 7-11
- Formal operations 11-adult

Younger students – short attention span; hands-on activities; Older students – beginning of hypothetical thinking.

Create **developmentally appropriate** instruction – relate to ages/stages of development.

Understand four **domains** of development.

Early intervention essential for **developmental delays.**

Play stages:
- Solitary
- Onlooker
- Parallel
- Associative
- Rough and tumble
- Cooperative

Provide integrated/thematic units—learning through **play.**

Construct own knowledge—no passive learning/ real life situations.

- Recognizes that positive and productive learning environments involve creating a culture of **high academic expectations,** equity throughout the learning community, and developmental responsiveness.

- Recognizes the importance of helping students in early childhood through grade 12 learn and apply **life skills** (e.g., decision-making skills, organizational skills, **goal-setting** skills, self-direction, workplace skills) to promote lifelong learning and active participation in **society.**

- Knows the rationale for appropriate middle-level education and how middle-level schools are structured to address the characteristics and needs of young adolescents

- Recognizes typical challenges for students during later childhood, adolescence, and young adulthood (e.g., **self-image,** physical appearance, eating disorders, feelings of rebelliousness, identity formation, educational and career decisions) and effective ways to help students address these challenges.

- Understands ways in which student involvement in risky behaviors (e.g., gang involvement, drug and alcohol use) impacts development and learning.

- Demonstrates knowledge of the importance of peers, peer acceptance, and conformity to **peer** group norms and expectations for adolescents; and understands the significance of **peer-related issues** for teaching and learning.

Stress importance of **high academic expectations** for all students.

Engage students in realistic problem-solving by applying **life skills.**

Provide **goal-setting** opportunities.

Promote social responsibility to **society.**

Validate student ideas/concerns.

Promote **self-image**/self-confidence/self-worth (no ability grouping).

Individualize when possible.

Adolescents—**peer** relationships and issues are important; need to belong is prevalent.

Peer acceptance is important.

Make connections between current skills and new skills.

COMPETENCY 2—Diversity

The teacher understands student diversity and knows how to plan learning experiences and design assessments that are responsive to differences among students and that promote all students' learning.

The beginning teacher:

- Demonstrates knowledge of students with diverse personal and social characteristics (e.g., those related to ethnicity, gender, language background, exceptionality) and the significance of student **diversity** for teaching, learning, and assessment.

- Accepts and **respects** students with diverse backgrounds and needs.

- Knows how to use diversity in the classroom and the **community** to enrich all students' learning experiences.

- Knows **strategies** for enhancing one's own understanding of students' diverse backgrounds and needs.

- Knows how to **plan** and **adapt lessons** to address students' varied backgrounds, skills, interests, and learning needs, including the needs of English language learners and students with disabilities.

- Understands cultural and socioeconomic **differences** (including differential access to technology) and knows how to plan instruction that is responsive to cultural and socioeconomic **differences** among students.

- Understands the instructional significance of **varied** student learning needs and preferences.

Understand uniqueness of individuals (**diversity**).

Teacher must model **respect** for all students to effect change in attitudes rather than trying to change family values.

Respect and celebrate differences.

Each cultural group has a broad range of strengths/interests/needs.

Nurture a sense of **community.**

One-to-one activities foster diverse students' communications.

Support positive expectations and role models as **strategies.**

Make **plans** that address student diversity **adapting lessons** by:

Direct involvement in cooperative learning

Heterogeneous grouping

Pursuing meaningful problems

Clearly defined behavior rules

Foster communications for **differences** in backgrounds:

Send notes home in home language.

Bring in involvement of all families.

Use **variety** of tasks for students with different ability levels to be successful.

Use variety of assessments but hold all to same standards.

Provide **variety** of activities for diverse learning needs.

COMPETENCY 3—Designing Instruction Based on Goals

The teacher understands procedures for designing effective and coherent instruction and assessment based on appropriate learning goals and objectives.

The beginning teacher:

- Understands the significance of the Texas Essential Knowledge and Skills (TEKS) and of prerequisite knowledge and skills in determining instructional goals and objectives.

- Uses appropriate criteria to evaluate the appropriateness of learning **goals** and **objectives** (e.g., clarity; relevance; significance; age-appropriateness; ability to be assessed; responsiveness to students' current skills and knowledge, background, needs, and interests; alignment with campus and district goals).

- Uses assessment to analyze students' strengths and needs, evaluate teacher effectiveness, and guide instructional planning for individuals and groups.

- Understands the connection between various components of the Texas statewide assessment program, the TEKS, and instruction, and analyzes data from state and other assessments using common statistical measures to help identify students' strengths and needs.

- Demonstrates knowledge of **various types of materials** and resources (including technological resources and resources outside the school) that may be used to enhance student learning and engagement and evaluates the appropriateness of specific materials and resources for use in particular situations, to address specific purposes, and to meet varied student needs.

- **Plans** lessons and structures units so that activities progress in a logical sequence and support stated instructional goals.

- Plans learning experiences that provide students with opportunities to explore content from integrated and varied perspectives (e.g., by presenting thematic units that incorporate different disciplines, providing **intradisciplinary** and **interdisciplinary** instruction, designing instruction that enables students to work cooperatively, providing multicultural learning experiences, prompting students to consider ideas from multiple viewpoints, encouraging students' application of knowledge and skills to the world beyond school).

- Allocates time appropriately within lessons and units, including providing adequate opportunities for students to engage in **reflection, self-assessment,** and closure.

Promote student ownership in the learning to accomplish goals.

First step—Define and clarify unit **goals** and objectives.

Have students set responsible **goals** for themselves.

Learning is enhanced by an understanding of **goals/ objectives** of instructional activities.

Individualize classroom instruction—don't teach to the majority.

Involve students in sharing ideas, backgrounds, and experiences.

Use a **variety of materials/**activities, including technology.

Careful **planning** = student success

Students make predictions and design questions.

Teachers work together to plan **intradisciplinary/interdisciplinary** units.

Foster active inquiry.

Students **reflect** on learning.

Encourage self-directed thinking, learning, and **self-assessment.**

Support collaborative exploration.

Foster critical thinking skills.

115

116

COMPETENCY 4—Engaging Instruction

The teacher understands learning processes and factors that impact student learning and demonstrates this knowledge by planning effective, engaging instruction and appropriate assessments.

The beginning teacher:

- Understands the role of learning theory in the instructional process and uses instructional strategies and appropriate technologies to facilitate student learning (e.g., **connecting** new **information** and ideas to prior knowledge, making learning meaningful and relevant to students).

- Understands that young children think concretely and rely primarily on motor and sensory input and direct experience for development of skills and knowledge, and uses this understanding to plan effective, **developmentally appropriate** learning experiences and assessments.

- Understands that the **middle-level years** are a transitional stage in which students may exhibit characteristics of both older and younger children, and that these are critical years for developing important skills and attitudes (e.g., working and getting along with others, appreciating diversity, making a commitment to continued schooling).

- Recognizes how characteristics of students at different developmental levels (e.g., limited attention span and need for physical activity and movement for younger children; importance of peers, search for identity, questioning of **values,** and exploration of long-term career and life goals for older students) impact teaching and learning.

- Applies knowledge of the implications for learning and instruction of the range of thinking abilities found among students in any one grade level and students' increasing ability over time to engage in abstract thinking and reasoning.

- Stimulates **reflection,** critical thinking, and inquiry among students (e.g., supports the concept of **play** as a valid vehicle for young children's learning; provides opportunities for young children to manipulate materials and to test ideas and hypotheses; engages students in structured, hands-on problem-solving activities that are challenging; encourages exploration and risk-taking; creates a learning community that promotes positive contributions, effective communication, and the respectful exchange of ideas).

- Enhances learning for students by providing age-appropriate instruction that encourages the use and refinement of **higher-order thinking skills** (e.g., prompting students to explore ideas from diverse perspectives; structuring active learning experiences involving cooperative learning, problem solving, open-ended questioning, and inquiry; promoting students' development of research skills).

- Incorporate student interests, real life situations, and authentic behavior.
- Draw on prior experiences/ **connect** old **information** to new.
- Provide **developmentally appropriate** instruction.
- Understand importance/confusion of **middle-level years.**
- Have students examine their personal **values.**
- Use student **reflection** as a learning strategy.
- Foster learning through **play.**
- Engage students in **higher-order thinking.**
- Use metacognitive prompts: **thinking about thinking.**

- Teaches, **models,** and monitors organizational and time-management skills at an age-appropriate level (e.g., establishing regular places for classroom toys and materials for young students, keeping related materials together, using organizational tools, using effective strategies for locating information, and organizing information systematically).

- Teaches, models, and monitors age-appropriate study skills (e.g., using **graphic organizers,** outlining, note-taking, summarizing, test-taking), and structures research projects appropriately (e.g., teaches students the steps in research, establishes checkpoints during research projects, helps students use time-management tools).

- Analyzes ways in which teacher behaviors (e.g., teacher expectations, student **grouping** practices, teacher-student interactions) impact student learning, and plans instruction and assessment that minimize the effects of negative factors and enhance all students' learning.

- Analyzes ways in which factors in the **home** and **community** (e.g., parent expectations, availability of community resources, community problems) impact student learning, and plans instruction and assessment with awareness of social and cultural factors to enhance all students' learning.

- Understands the importance of self-directed learning and plans instruction and assessment that promote students' **motivation** and their sense of ownership of and responsibility for their own learning.

- Analyzes ways in which various **teacher roles** (e.g., **facilitator,** lecturer) and student roles (e.g., active learner, observer, group participant) impact student learning.

- Incorporates students' different approaches to learning (e.g., auditory, visual, tactile, kinesthetic) into instructional practices.

- **Model** by showing correct behaviors.

- Understand effectiveness of pictures/drawings as **graphic organizers.**

- Provide flexible **grouping** for students' self-esteem/competence.

- Understand that students from lower SES **homes** may perform at a lower level than upper SES students.

- Use guest speakers from the **community.**

- Promote self-**motivation;** intrinsic/extrinsic **motivation.**

- Know **teacher roles:** instructor, **facilitator,** problem solver, resource person, curriculum developer, representative of the school.

- Teacher as a **facilitator** provides structure and answers questions as needed

- Promote student ownership and responsibility for learning.

- Promote self-monitoring and reflection.

- Allow student choice/control when possible.

COMPETENCY 5—Classroom Climate

The teacher knows how to establish a classroom climate that fosters learning, equity, excellence and uses this knowledge to create a physical and emotional environment that is safe and productive.

The beginning teacher:

- Uses knowledge of the unique characteristics and needs of students at different developmental levels to establish a positive, productive classroom environment (e.g., encourages cooperation and sharing among younger students; provides middle-level students with opportunities to collaborate with peers; encourages older students' respect for the **community** and the people in it).

- Establishes a classroom climate that emphasizes **collaboration** and supportive interactions, **respect** for diversity and individual differences, and active engagement in learning by all students.

- Analyzes ways in which teacher–student interactions and **interactions** among students impact classroom climate and student learning and development.

- Presents instruction in ways that communicate the teacher's enthusiasm for learning.

- Uses a variety of means to convey **high expectations** for all students.

- Knows characteristics of physical spaces that are safe and productive for learning, recognizes the benefits and limitations of various arrangements of furniture in the classroom, and applies strategies for organizing the physical environment to ensure physical accessibility and facilitate learning in various instructional contexts.

- Creates a safe, nurturing, and inclusive classroom environment that addresses students' **emotional** needs and respects students' rights and dignity.

Provide **climate** of support and inquiry.

Promote active engagement/lifelong pursuit of learning.

Promote ownership of and membership in functioning school and **community.**

Collaborative learning:

Clarify procedures and requirements

Set goals/purposes

Monitor/intervene when necessary

Encourage cooperation, leadership, and mutual **respect.**

Foster **interactions** with productive group work—use student experts.

Allow no single-gender groups.

High Expectations:

Provide flexible grouping/avoid labels

Express confidence in students' abilities

Help reluctant learners set/ achieve goals

Promote positive social/**emotional** atmosphere.

Give students multiple chances for success.

Validate student concerns/questions.

Teacher models problem-solving behaviors.

Provide climate of trust and respect/use of student names.

COMPETENCY 6—Managing Student Behavior

The teacher understands strategies for creating an organized and productive learning environment and for managing student behavior.

The beginning teacher:

- Analyzes the effects of classroom **routines** and **procedures** on student learning and knows how to establish and implement age-appropriate routines and procedures to promote an organized and productive learning environment.

- Demonstrates an understanding of how young children function in groups and designs **group** activities that reflect a realistic understanding of the extent of young children's ability to collaborate with others.

- Organizes and manages group activities to work together cooperatively and productively, assume responsible roles, and develop collaborative skills and individual accountability.

- Recognizes the importance of creating a schedule for young children that balances restful and **active** movement activities and that provides large blocks of time for play, projects, and learning centers.

- Schedules activities and manages **time** in ways that maximize student learning, including using effective procedures to manage **transitions;** to manage **materials,** supplies, and technology; and to coordinate the performance of non-instructional duties (e.g., taking attendance) with instructional activities.

- Uses technological tools to perform administrative tasks such as taking attendance, maintaining **grade books,** and facilitating communication.

- Works with volunteers and paraprofessionals to enhance and enrich instruction and applies procedures for monitoring the performance of volunteers and paraprofessionals in the classroom.

- Applies theories and techniques related to managing and monitoring student **behavior.**

- Demonstrates awareness of appropriate behavior standards and expectations for students at various developmental levels.

- Applies effective procedures for managing student behavior and for promoting appropriate behavior and ethical work habits (e.g., academic integrity) in the classroom (e.g., communicating high and realistic **behavior expectations,** involving students in developing **rules** and procedures, establishing clear consequences for inappropriate behavior, enforcing behavior standards consistently, encouraging students to monitor their own behavior and to use conflict resolution skills, responding appropriately to various types of behavior).

- Establish/maintain **routines.**
  Beginning of school year—establish **procedures.**
- Provide shorter large **group** times for younger students.

- Provide **active** involvement of younger students with hands-on activities.
- Maximize learning **time.**
- Reflect on **time** management skills.
- Specify outcome/product for group work, allowing planning, rehearsing, evaluating **time.**
- Plan **transitions.**
- Make **materials** accessible.
- Spreadsheets for **grade books** provide for efficient grade calculation with weights.

- Establish and maintain standards of **behavior.**

- Clarify **behavioral expectations** and consequences.
- State consistent **rules** positively with student input.
- Seek student input when establishing **rules** for behavior.
- Actively engage students in meaningful/productive learning.
- Set up physical environment that is conducive to achieving goals.
- Break large projects into pieces using several deadlines along the way.
- Provide fair/consistent discipline management plan applied the same to all students.

COMPETENCY 7—Communication

The teacher understands and applies principles and strategies for communicating effectively in varied teaching and learning contexts.

The beginning teacher:

- Demonstrates clear, accurate communication in the teaching and learning process and uses language that is appropriate to students' ages, interests, and backgrounds.
  - Vary methods of conveying concepts, especially when students don't understand.
  - Provide teacher modeling.
  - Use thoughtful **questioning.**

- Engages in skilled questioning and leads effective student discussions, including using **questioning** and discussion to engage all students in exploring content; extends students' knowledge; and fosters active student inquiry, higher order thinking, **problem solving,** and productive, supportive interactions, including appropriate wait time.
  - Use probing, prompting, clues, and simpler but related **questions.**
  - Promote risk taking and **problem solving.**
  - Model expectations by discussions and comparisons of poor work to well done work.
  - Elicit needed clarification.

- Communicates directions, explanations, and procedures effectively and uses strategies for adjusting communication to enhance student understanding (e.g., by providing **examples,** simplifying complex ideas, using appropriate communication tools).
  - Use familiar **examples.**
  - Facilitate factual recall, divergent thinking, stimulate curiosity.

- Practices effective **communication** techniques and interpersonal skills (including both **verbal** and **nonverbal** skills and electronic communication) for meeting specified goals in various contexts.
  - Focus teacher–student **communication** on internal development of student.
  - Use effective **verbal, nonverbal,** and media communication.
  - Be sensitive to **nonverbal** cues given and received.
  - Be a reflective listener — restate student response.
  - Use simplifying and restating.
  - Consider purpose/audience intended.
  - Help students set responsible goals.
  - Cultural aspects of communication will vary.
  - Elicit different levels of thinking.

COMPETENCY 8—Active Learning

The teacher provides appropriate instruction that actively engages students in the learning process.

The beginning teacher:

- Employs various instructional techniques (e.g., discussion, inquiry), varies teacher and student **roles** in the instructional process, and provides instruction that promotes intellectual involvement and active student engagement and learning.

  Teacher **roles**—instructor, facilitator, coach, audience, diagnostician.

  Be aware that learning occurs in and out of classroom.

- Applies **various** strategies to promote student engagement and learning (e.g., by structuring lessons effectively, using flexible instructional groupings, pacing lessons flexibly in response to student needs, including wait time).

  Provide **variety** of instructional strategies:
  Real-world/authentic problems
  Interdisciplinary instruction
  Cooperative learning
  Discovery learning
  Open-ended questions
  Heterogeneous groups

- Presents content to students in ways that are **relevant** and meaningful and that link with students' prior **knowledge** and experience.

  Promote **relevance** to students' own needs, interests, and background **knowledge.**

  Practice group decision-making skills.

- Applies criteria for **evaluating** the appropriateness of instructional activities, materials, resources, and technologies for students with varied characteristics and needs.

  Promote higher order thinking, comparison, analysis, and **evaluation.**

- Engages in continuous **monitoring** of instructional effectiveness.

  Constantly **monitor**/adjust strategies in response to feedback.

- Applies knowledge of different types of motivation (i.e., internal, external) and factors affecting student motivation.

  Focus, organize, conduct investigations, communicate reasoning processes and conclusions.

- Employs effective **motivational strategies** and encourages students' self-motivation.

  Motivational strategies:
  Choose project presentation methods for creative expression (art, music, drama, multimedia)
  Be successful in meaningful and challenging activities

  Help students become independent thinkers/problem solvers through inquiry.
  Advantages of cooperative learning teams:
  Combine ability and experience
  High achievers deepen own understanding
  Students learn to appreciate others unique talents/skills

121

COMPETENCY 9—Technology

The teacher incorporates the effective use of technology to plan, organize, deliver, and evaluate instruction for all students.

The beginning teacher:

- Demonstrates knowledge of basic terms and concepts of current technology (e.g., hardware, software applications and functions, input/output devices, networks).

  Computers should be used to support regular classroom content rather than as a separate lab activity for drill and practice.

- Understands issues related to the appropriate use of technology in society and follows guidelines for the legal and ethical use of technology and digital information (e.g., privacy guidelines, **copyright laws**, acceptable use policies).

  Web sources should be cited just as printed materials to observe **copyright laws.**

- Applies procedures for acquiring, analyzing, and **evaluating** electronic information (e.g., locating information on networks, accessing and manipulating information from secondary storage and remote devices, using online help and other documentation, evaluating electronic information for accuracy and validity).

  When using the Internet:

  FIRST make sure the students know how to **evaluate** web resources to determine the author/sponsor and the purpose of the website.

  A SECOND step to promote information literacy is to examine other perspectives from reliable sources. (Personal testimonies from individuals may not be reliable.)

- Knows how to use task-appropriate tools and procedures to **synthesize** knowledge, create and modify solutions, and evaluate results to support the work of individuals and groups in problem-solving situations and project-based learning activities (e.g., planning, creating, and **editing** word processing documents, spreadsheet documents, and databases; using graphic tools; participating in electronic communities as learner, initiator, and contributor; sharing information through online communication).

  Use various technology tools such as digital and video cameras, PowerPoint presentations, email to **synthesize** (put together) new information/concepts or confirm/reinforce existing knowledge.

  Edit your work—don't depend entirely on spell check.

- Knows how to use **productivity tools** to communicate information in various formats (e.g., slide show, multimedia presentation, newsletter) and applies procedures for publishing information in various ways (e.g., printed copy, monitor display, Internet document, video).

  Use **productivity tools**—software to increase a teacher's effectiveness such as a grade book program, spreadsheet, puzzle maker, test generator, etc.

- Knows how to incorporate the effective use of current technology; use technology applications in problem-solving and decision-making situations; implement activities that emphasize collaboration and teamwork; and use **developmentally appropriate** instructional practices, activities, and materials to integrate the Technology Applications TEKS into the curriculum.

  Allow students to explore computer for a **developmentally appropriate** activity.

  Rubrics should be used to **evaluate** technology projects and to focus student efforts, reducing teacher subjectivity.

- Knows how to **evaluate** students' technologically produced products and projects using established criteria related to design, content delivery, audience, and relevance to assignment.

  Evaluate by using a performance assessment—have student perform the skill on the computer.

- Identifies and addresses equity issues related to the use of technology.

  Technology tends to be a motivational tool.

122

COMPETENCY 10—Assessment

The teacher monitors student performance and achievement; provides students with timely, high-quality feedback; and responds flexibly to promote learning for all students.

The beginning teacher:

- Demonstrates knowledge of the characteristics, uses, advantages, and limitations of **various** assessment methods and strategies, including technological methods and methods that reflect real-world applications.

- Creates assessments that are congruent with instructional goals and **objectives** and communicates assessment **criteria** and standards to students based on high expectations for learning.

- Uses appropriate language and formats to provide students with timely, effective **feedback** that is accurate, constructive, substantive, and specific.

- Knows how to promote students' ability to use **feedback** and **self-assessment** to guide and enhance their own learning.

- Responds flexibly to various situations (e.g., lack of student engagement in an activity, the occurrence of an unanticipated learning opportunity) and adjusts instructional approaches based on **ongoing assessment** of student performance.

First step is to define learner outcomes.

Use a **variety** of types of assessment (formal and informal) covering a broad range of factors to determine student grades.

Provide clearly stated **objectives** to help students to judge their own work.

Involve students in creating evaluation **criteria.**

For low-achieving students, **feedback** should be focused on progress over time not on comparisons to other students.

Rubrics encourage self-reflection.

Regular/constructive **feedback** is essential.

Self-assessment develops reflective and critical attitude toward one's own work, but teacher assessments based on standards should carry more weight for grading.

Evaluate group projects by:

   Peer assessment

   Self-assessment

   Teacher observation

   Rubrics

Ongoing assessment through the year ensures developmentally appropriate instruction.

Multiple approaches/utilizing "teachable moments" draw in unmotivated students.

Use **assessment** to:

   Understand learners and their needs

   Monitor instruction effectiveness

   Shape instruction

COMPETENCY 11—Family Involvement

The teacher understands the importance of family involvement in children's education and knows how to interact and communicate effectively with families.

The beginning teacher:

- Applies knowledge of appropriate ways (including electronic communication) to work and **communicate** effectively with families in various situations.

  - Establish ongoing, two-way **communication** with home.
  - Get parents' help in understanding/evaluating child's behavior/performance.

- Engages families, **parents, guardians,** and other legal caregivers in various aspects of the educational program.

  - Provide parents with opportunities for **parent/guardian** participation in school events.

- **Interacts** appropriately with all families, including those that have diverse characteristics, backgrounds, and needs.

  - Create activities that are built on natural **interactions** within the family.
  - Know that problems affect student learning.
  - Invite parents to speak in class to establish student awareness between meaningful classroom learning and future job opportunities.

- Communicates effectively with families on a **regular** basis (e.g., to share information about students' progress) and responds to their concerns.

  - Provide **regular** updates to parents.
  - Promote students' sense of social responsibility.

- Conducts effective conferences with parents, guardians, and other legal caregivers.

  - School is a part of the larger **community** so help students understand value/stradi-tions of community.
  - Use **community** strengths and resources to foster student growth.

- Effectively uses family support resources (e.g., **community,** interagency) to enhance family involvement in student learning.

  - Recognize problems in the **community:** drugs, gangs, racism, crime, unemployment, poverty.
  - Promote **community** appreciation of school.
  - Create a strong relationship of trust with parent/guardian by personal contact.
  - Effective parent/teacher partnerships foster student's learning and well-being.

124

COMPETENCY 12—Professional Development

The teacher enhances professional knowledge and skills by effectively interacting with other members of the educational community and participating in various types of professional activities.

The beginning teacher:

- Interacts appropriately with other professionals in the school community (e.g., vertical teaming, horizontal teaming, team teaching, mentoring).

- Maintains supportive, **cooperative** relationships with professional **colleagues** and **collaborates** to support students' learning and to achieve campus and district goals.

- Knows the roles and responsibilities of **specialists** and other professionals at the building and district levels (e.g., department chairperson, principal, board of trustees, curriculum coordinator, technology coordinator, **special education professional**).

- Understands the value of participating in school activities and contributes to school and district (e.g., by participating in decision making and problem solving, sharing ideas and expertise, serving on **committees**, volunteering to participate in events and projects).

- Uses resources and support systems effectively (e.g., mentors, **service centers**, state initiatives, universities) to address professional development needs.

- Recognizes characteristics, goals, and procedures associated with teacher appraisal and uses appraisal results to improve teaching skills.

- Works productively with supervisors, mentors, and other **colleagues** to address issues and to enhance professional knowledge and skills.

- Understands and uses **professional** development resources (e.g., mentors and other support systems, conferences, online resources, workshops, journals, professional associations, coursework) to enhance knowledge, pedagogical skills, and **technological** expertise.

- Engages in **reflection** and **self-assessment** to identify strengths, challenges, and potential problems; improve teaching performance; and achieve professional goals.

- Promote own professional growth.

- When communicating with other professionals, make sure goals are clear.

- Seek **collaboration** through the Internet for motivational lesson plans.

- Teachers should volunteer to do demonstration lessons for **colleagues**.

- Work **cooperatively** with other teachers, mentors, **specialists**, and school personnel.

- Seek advice FIRST from **special education professionals** in diagnosing possible learning disabilities.

- Work toward consensus as a **committee** member.

- Teachers should be aware of state-funded resources and professional development opportunities at regional education **service centers**.

- Seek help from professional staff members on serious student problems beyond the scope of classroom learning.

- Collaborate with **colleagues** to promote learning, explore ideas, and accomplish educational goals.

- Observe **colleagues** who use effective methods in the classroom and for classroom management.

- Actively seek out opportunities to grow **professionally** and with **technology**.

- Use **reflection** and **self-assessment** on biases, school mission, and teaching methods.

Cut along dotted line

126

COMPETENCY 13—Legal/Ethical Requirements

The teacher understands and adheres to legal and ethical requirements for educators and is knowledgeable of the structure of education in Texas.

The beginning teacher:

- Knows legal requirements for educators (e.g., those related to **special education**, students' and families' rights, student discipline, equity, **child abuse**) and adheres to **legal** guidelines in education-related situations.

- Knows and adheres to legal and ethical requirements regarding the use of educational resources and technologies (e.g., **copyright, fair use,** data security, privacy, acceptable use policies).

- Applies knowledge of ethical guidelines for educators in Texas (e.g., those related to **confidentiality,** interactions with students and others in the school community), including policies and procedures described in the *Code of Ethics and Standard Practices for Texas Educators.*

- Follows procedures and requirements for maintaining accurate **student records.**
- Understands the importance of and adheres to required procedures for administering state- and district-mandated assessments.
- Uses knowledge of the structure of the state education system, including relationships among **campus,** local, and state components, to seek information and assistance.

- **Advocates** for **students** and for the profession in various situations.

Initiate **special education** referral when other classroom strategies fail.

Report suspected **child abuse** to proper local or state authority within 48 hours.

Follow field trip **legalities:** permission from administration and from parent/guardian.

Strictly observe **copyright** and **fair use** laws: for educational purposes, limited spontaneous use is allowed, but repetitive use is not allowed.

Observe student **confidentiality:** share grades only with child, parent/guardian, or education staff directly involved with student's educational program.

Code of Ethics: All students must participate without advantage or benefits to diverse groups.

Allow each student to achieve potential through appropriate instruction.

Keep back-up of **student records.**

Teachers are directly responsible to and must consult with the **campus** principal first when seeking advice or assistance.

Campus decision-making committee (SBDM) plans strategies and promotes district goals for student achievement.

Speak out to other professionals for the good of the students as their **advocate.**

Effective **advocates** understand children's/family needs.

B

Practice Test Analysis Charts

These charts help you focus on the right answers for each competency.

It is important for you to summarize in your own words, and not copy word for word from the test, both the questions and the correct answers. This step is critical in making the material your own in order to pass the test.

After looking at all of the correct answers for a compentency, create keyword phrases for yourself to help you remember the kinds of answers that are correct for each competency on the test.

Cut along dotted line

Competency 1
Main Idea:

Question No.	Summary of what question is asking:	Keyword Phrases: / Summary of correct answer:

Competency 2
Main Idea:

Question No.	Summary of what question is asking:	Keyword Phrases:	Summary of correct answer:

Cut along dotted line

Competency 3
Main Idea:

Keyword Phrases:

Question No.	Summary of what question is asking:	Summary of correct answer:

Competency 4
Main Idea:

Keyword Phrases:

Question No.	Summary of what question is asking:	Summary of correct answer:

Competency 5
Main Idea:

Keyword Phrases:

Question No.	Summary of what question is asking:	Summary of correct answer:

Cut along dotted line

Competency 6
Main Idea:

Question No.	Summary of what question is asking:	Keyword Phrases: Summary of correct answer:

133

Competency 7
Main Idea:

Question No.	Summary of what question is asking:	Keyword Phrases: Summary of correct answer:

Competency 8
Main Idea:

Keyword Phrases:

Question No.	Summary of what question is asking:	Summary of correct answer:

Competency 9
Main Idea:

Question No.	Summary of what question is asking:	Keyword Phrases: Summary of correct answer:

Cut along dotted line

Competency 10
Main Idea:

Keyword Phrases:

Question No.	Summary of what question is asking:	Summary of correct answer:

137

Competency 11
Main Idea:

Keyword Phrases:

Question No.	Summary of what question is asking:	Summary of correct answer:

Cut along dotted line

Competency 12
Main Idea:

Question No.	Summary of what question is asking:	Keyword Phrases:	Summary of correct answer:

139

Cut along dotted line

Competency 13
Main Idea:

Keyword Phrases:

Question No.	Summary of what question is asking:	Summary of correct answer:

Index

A

Abbreviations exercise, 99–100
Academic goals, 70
Acceptable use policy (AUP), 72
Accommodation, 32, 37
Accountability, 82
Acculturation, 32
Achievement, 61
Achievement test, 76
Active learning, 24, 65–71, 121
 best practices, 65–66
 cooperative learning, 69–71
 environments and abilities, 66
 instruction models, 66–69
Active participation, promoting,
 20
Activities, age-appropriate, 10
Administrators, 82
Admission review and dismissal
 (ARD), 90
Adolescence, defined, 32
Adolescent development, 39
Advanced organizer, 15
Advocate, teacher as, 4
Affective domain, 32, 43
Age appropriate, 32
Algorithm, 61
Alternative assessment, 76
Alternative Education Program
 (AEP), 50
Analogy, 15
Analysis, 42
Answer, intent of, 9
Application, 42
Aptitude test, 76
Assertive discipline, 54
Assessment, 3, 75–77, 123
 alternative, 76
 authentic, 61, 76
 best practices, 75
 evaluation *versus*, 75–76

formal, 76
formative, 61
informal, 76
needs, 61
performance, 61, 76–77
summative, 61
test construction, 77
types, 76–77
Assimilation, 32, 37
Assisted learning, 37
Associative play, 38
At-risk, 82
Authentic assessment, 61, 76
Authoritarian, 50
Authority, 54
Autonomy *versus* shame/doubt
 stage, 38

B

Basic needs, 55
Behavior contract, 55
Behavior modification theory, 55
Behavior problems
 contracts for, 55
 managing, 55–56
 self-discipline model, 55
 serious misbehavior, 55
Bilingual education, 91
Biracial, 32
Bloom, Benjamin, 42
Bloom's domains for objectives,
 42–43
 affective, 43
 cognitive, 42–43
 psychomotor, 43
Bookmark/favorite, 72
Browser, 73

C

Campus improvement plan
 (CIP), 87

Campus improvement team
 (CIT), 87
Central themes, of disciplines, 2
Cephalocaudal development, 37
Chain of command, 10, 21
Charter school, 82
Child development, 36–39
 cognitive, 36
 emotional, 36
 physical, 36
 social, 36
Classroom climate, 49–58, 52–53,
 118
 best practices, 52
 defined, 50
 environment, 52
 expectations for, 52
 Maslow's hierarchy of needs,
  52–53
Classroom discipline, 20
Classroom management, 20, 50,
 53–54
 assertive discipline, 54
 behavior problems, 55–56
 conflict resolution, 56–57
 factors of, 53–54
 management style, 54
 operant conditioning, 55
 reality therapy, 55
 room arrangement, 57
Classroom philosophy, adopting
 appropriate, 2
Code of Ethics for Teachers in
 Texas, 93–96
Cognitive development, 36
 concrete operations, 37
 formal operations, 37
 Piaget, Jean, 37
 preoperational, 37
 sensorimotor, 37
 Vygotsky, Lev, 37

Cognitive domain, 32, 42–43
  analysis, 42
  application, 42
  comprehension, 42
  evaluation, 43
  knowledge, 42
  synthesis, 43
Cognitive learning styles, 46
Collaboration (collaborate), 15
  with colleagues, 20
  horizontal teaching, 86
  integration teaching, 86
  mentoring, 86
  professional development
    and, 86
  team teaching, 86
  vertical teaching, 86
Collaborative instruction, 20
Collaborative team, of teachers, 5
Communication, 63–65, 120
  best practices, 63
  discussions, 64
  effective, 63–64
  expressive, 64
  informative, 64
  inquiry, 4
  via Internet, 85
  learner-centered, 4
  media, 4
  narrative, 64
  nonverbal, 4
  persuasive, 64
  praise, 64
  questioning techniques, 64–65
  verbal, 4
  word associations, 26
Community
  learner-centered, 2
  school, 86–87
  support, 88
  ties with school, 4
Compensatory education, 82
Competencies
  1, 36–39, 112–13, 128
  2, 39–41, 114, 129
  3, 41–44, 115, 130
  4, 44–47, 116–17, 131
  5, 12, 52–53, 118
  6, 53–57, 119, 133
  7, 63–65, 120, 134
  8, 65–71, 121, 135
  9, 72–75, 122, 136
  10, 75–77, 123, 137
  11, 84–85, 124, 138
  12, 86–89, 125, 139
  13, 89–96, 126, 140

Competitive environment, 66
Comprehension, 42
Compulsory education, 82
Computer assisted instruction
  (CAI), 73
Computer graphics, 73
Computer use, skills, 73
Concrete operations stage, 37
Conduct, 54
Conferences, parent-teacher,
  84–85
Confidentiality, 82
Conflict, types of, 56
Conflict resolution, 50, 56–57
  conflict, types of, 56
  goal of, 56
  strategies, 56
Consequences, 50
  extinction, 55
  punishment, 55
  reinforcement, 55
Constructivism, 32
Content, 54
Content, of domain I, 36–48
  diversity, 39–41
  human growth and
    development, 36–39
  instruction, designing, 41–44
  instruction, engaging, 44–47
Continuing professional
  education (CPE), 88
Contract, behavior, 55
Convergent questions, 65
Cooperation, 24
Cooperative environment, 66
Cooperative learning, 4, 9, 24
  benefits, 69
  as best practice, 20
  elements of, 69
  groups, 70–71
  instruction models, 68–69
  promoting, 20
  teacher's role, 69–70
  teaching, 70
  word associations, 26
Cooperative play, 39
Copyright guidelines, 92–93
  fair use, 93
  market value, 93
  spontaneity test, 93
Copyright laws, 74–75
Covenant, 54
Creative thinking, 20
Creativity, 3
Criterion-referenced test, 76
Critical thinking, 3, 15

as best practice, 20
  fostering, 20
  promoting, 66
Cross-cultural experiences, 3
Cues
  nonverbal, 63, 64
  verbal, 63
Cultural diversity, celebrating,
  as best practice, 20
Cultural heritage, accepting, 3
Culturally relevant teaching, 40
Cultural pluralism, 32
Culture, 40
  defined, 32
Curriculum, 15

D
Database, 73
Deductive reasoning, 61
Desktop publishing, 73
Development, 32
  adolescent, 39
  child, 36–39
  physical, 37–38, 39
Developmentally appropriate, 32
Diagnostic test, 76
Direct instruction models, 66
Disabilities, types of, 91–92
Discipline
  assertive, 54
  classroom, 20
  defined, 50
Discourse, 15
Discovery, 9, 20
  learning, 61
Discussions, effective, 64
Distance education, 72
Distracters, eliminating, 8, 10
Divergent questions, 65
Diversity, 39–41, 114
  appreciation for, 20
  best practices, 39–40
  celebrating, 9, 20
  defined, 32, 40
  multicultural education, 40
  word associations, 26
Domain, 15
Domain I, of PPR, 31–48
  content, 36–48
  vocabulary, 32–33
Domain II, of PPR, 49–58
Domain III, of PPR, 59–79
  standards assessed, 59–60
Domain IV, of PPR, 81–98
  standard assessed, 81
Drill and practice, 74

E
Eclectic, 15
Effective communication, 63–64
  nonverbal cues, 63
  probing, 63
  prompting, 63
  verbal cues, 63
Effective discussions, 64
Effective praise, 64
Egocentric, 32
E-mail, 74
Emotional development, 36
  autonomy *versus*
    shame/doubt, 38
  identity *versus* role confusion,
    38
  industry *versus* inferiority, 38
  initiative *versus* guilt, 38
  interdependent stages of, 38
  intimacy *versus* isolation, 38
  trust *versus* mistrust, 38
Emotional tasks, 38
Empathetic listening, 61
Empower (empowerment), 15
English as a Second Language
    (ESL), 91
English Language Learners
    (ELL), 24, 91
Environments
  abilities and, 66
  classroom, 52
  competitive, 66
  cooperative, 66
  diversity and, 41
  individualistic, 66
  learner-centered, 20
  positive, 20
  safe, 10, 20
Equity, in access to technology,
    72
Equity in excellence for all
    learners, 3–4, 6
  cross-cultural experiences, 3
  cultural heritage, 3
  interests, 3
  learning styles, 3
Erikson, Erik, 38
  emotional development and,
    38
Ethical principles, 5, 89–96, 126
  best practices, 89
  code of ethics, 93–96
Ethics, 82
Ethnic group, 32
Ethnicity, 32, 40
Ethnocentrism, 32

Evaluation, 43
  assessment *versus*, 75–76
  holistic, 61
Exercise answer keys, 107–9
Expectations, high, 20, 24, 52
Experimentation, encouraging,
    21
Explicit, 15
Expressive communication
    technique, 64
Extinction, 55
Extrinsic motivation, 71

F
Fair use, copyright law, 93
Family Educational Rights and
    Privacy Act (FERPA), 91
Family involvement, 84–85, 124
  best practices, 84
  parent-teacher conferences,
    84–85
Feedback, 16
Field-dependent, 32, 46
Field-independent, 32, 46
Fine motor skills, 39
Flashcard exercise, 19
Formal assessment, 76
Formal operations stage, 37
Formative assessment, 61, 76
Free, appropriate public
    education (FAPE), 89

G
Gardner's multiple intelligences,
    46–47
Gender, 40
General vocabulary, 15–18
  exercise, 17–18
Global society, 4
Goals, professional, 4
Good teaching practices, 24–25
Graphic organizer, 16
Gross motor skills, 39
Grouping
  heterogeneous, 10
  homogeneous, 16, 66
Groupware, 74
Guided participation, 37
Guided practice, 32

H
Hardware, 72
Heterogeneous grouping, 10, 24
  defined, 16
  use of, 20
Higher-level thinking skills, 9, 32

Higher order thinking
  as best practice, 20
  fostering, 20
Highlighting exercise, 47–48,
    57–58, 78–79, 97–98
Holistic evaluation, 61
Home language survey, 91
Homework, 44
  guidelines, 44
Homogeneous grouping, 16, 66
Horizontal teaming, 86
Human growth and
    development, 36–39, 112–13
  best practices, 36
  child development, 36–39
Hyperlink, 72
Hypermedia, 72
Hyperstudio, 72
Hypertext, 72

I
Identity, search for, 38
Identity *versus* role confusion
    stage, 38
Implicit, 16
Impulsivity, 16
Inclusion, 82
Indirect instruction models,
    67–68
Indispensable information,
    15–29
  common verbs, 28–29
  flashcard exercise, 19
  general vocabulary, 15–16,
    17–18
  good teaching practices, 24–25
  research-based practices,
    20–21, 22–23
  word associations, 26–27
Individual education plan (IEP),
    89, 90
  classroom modifications, 90
Individualistic environment, 66
Individuals with Disabilities
    Education Act (IDEA), 89
  free, appropriate public
    education (FAPE), 89
  individual education plan
    (IEP), 89, 90
  least restrictive environment
    (LRE), 89, 90
  zero reject, 89
Inductive reasoning, 61
Industry *versus* inferiority stage,
    38
Informal assessment, 76

Information, indispensable,
  15–29
Informative communication
  technique, 64
Initiative *versus* guilt stage, 38
Input device, 72
Inquiry, 61
Inquiry teaching method, 4
Instruction, 16
  direct, 67
  effective, 21
  indirect, 67–68
  learner-centered, 2–3
  models, 66–69
Instruction, designing, 41–44,
  115
  best practices, 41–42
  Bloom's domains, 42–44
Instruction, engaging, 44–45,
  116–17
  best practices, 44–45
  metacognition, 45
  reflective teaching, 45
Instructional effectiveness,
  measuring, 76
Instructional strategy, 61
Integration teaming, 86
Interdependent stages, of
  development, 38
Interdisciplinary unit, 32
Interests, recognizing, 3
Internalize, 16
Internet, communication via, 85
Intimacy *versus* isolation stage,
  38
Intrinsic motivation, 71

J
Jigsaw, 68–69

K
Keywords, in questions, 8, 10
Kinesthetic (tactile) learners, 32
Knowledge
  current, 2
  defined, 42
  learner-centered, 1, 2
  prior, 20
KWL, 32

L
Language, 40
Leadership, as best practice, 20
Learner-centered
  communication, 4, 5
  community, 2

defined, 16
environment, 20
instruction, 2–3, 5
knowledge, 2, 5
professional development,
  4–5, 6
Learner-centered philosophy, 8
  age-appropriate activities, 10
  applying, 9–10
  chain of command, 10
  cooperative learning, 9
  discovery and, 9
  diversity, 9
  environment, safe, 10
  heterogeneous grouping, 10
  higher-level thinking skills, 9
  mistakes, learning from, 9
  special education students
    and, 10
  as student-centered, 9
Learner-centered proficiencies
  for teachers, 1–5
  Equity and excellence for all
    learners, 1, 6
  Learner-centered
    communication, 1, 6
  Learner-centered instruction,
    1, 5
  Learner-centered knowledge,
    1, 5
  Learner-centered professional
    development, 1, 6
*Learner-Centered Schools for Texas:
  A Vision of Texas Educators,* 1
Learning
  active, 24
  assisted, 37
  center, 50
  cooperative, 4, 9, 20, 24
  discovery, 61
  as life-long process, 3
  as lifetime pursuit, 21
  as process, 24
  project, 16
  rote, 16
  self-directed, 16
  student ownership of, 20
  vicarious, 16
Learning styles, 44
  cognitive, 46
  field-dependent, 46
  field-independent, 46
  multiple intelligences and,
    46–47
  recognizing, 3

Least restrictive environment
  (LRE), 89, 90
Left brain/hemisphere, 46
Legal requirements, 89–96, 126
  admission review and
    dismissal (ARD), 90
  best practices, 89
  copyright guidelines, 92–93
  disabilities/special needs,
    91–92
  Individuals with Disabilities
    Education Act (IDEA), 89
  placement, 91
  principles, 89–92
Lesson plans, 43
Limited English Proficient (LEP),
  91
Linking, 72
Listening, empathetic, 61
Local area network (LAN), 72

M
Management, classroom, 20
Management style, 54
  authority, 54
  conduct, 54
  content, 54
  covenant, 54
  power, 54
  three Cs, 54
Maslow's hierarchy of needs, 52
  higher growth needs, 53
  lower level, 52–53
Mastery, 76
Maturation, 32
Media teaching techniques, 4
Melting pot theory, 32
Mentor/mentoring, 82, 86, 89
Metacognition, 21, 33, 45
Mission, school, 4
Mistakes, learning from, 21
Mnemonic, 61
Modality, 16
Modeling
  defined, 33
  reflection, 45
  respectful behavior, 3
Modification, 82
Motivation, 65–71
  best practices, 65–66
  developing, 20
  extrinsic, 71
  intrinsic, 71
  techniques, 71
Motor skills
  fine, 39

gross, 39
Multicultural education, 40
  implementation methods,
    40–41
Multimedia, 74
Multiple intelligences, 46–47
  bodily-kinesthetic, 46
  interpersonal, 46
  intrapersonal, 46
  logical-mathematical, 46
  muscial-rhythmic, 46
  naturalist, 46
  verbal-linguistic, 46
  visual-spatial, 46
Multiracial, 32

N
Narrative communication
    technique, 64
Needs assessment, 61
Negative reinforcement, 55
Network interface card (NIC), 73
Nonverbal cues, 61, 63, 64
Nonverbal teaching techniques,
    4
Norm-referenced test, 76
Novice, 82

O
Objectives, writing, 42
Objectivity, 16
Observation, 77
Onlooker play, 38
Operant conditioning, 55
Output device, 73

P
Paradigm, 16
Parallel play, 38
Parent-teacher conferences,
    84–85
  Internet communication, 85
  jargon, eliminating, 85
Participation, guided, 37
Pedagogy, 16
Pedagogy and Professional
    Responsibilities (PPR)
    TExES exams, 1, 9
  common verbs on, 28–29
  domain I, 31–48
  domain II, 49–58
  domain III, 59–78
  domain IV, 81–98
  exact wording, from
    proficiencies, 2
Peer tutoring, 71

Percentile score, 61
Performance assessment, 61, 76
Permissive, 50
Personal identity, developing,
    38
Persuasive communication
    technique, 64
Philosophy
  classroom, 2
  learner-centered, 8, 9–10
Philosophy, test, 1–6
Physical development, 36, 37–38,
    39
  cephalocaudal, 37
  proximodistal, 38
Piaget, Jean, 37
  cognitive development stages,
    37
Placement, determining, 91
Play development, stages of,
    38–39
  associative, 38
  cooperative, 39
  onlooker, 38
  parallel, 38
  rough and tumble, 38
  solitary, 38
Portfolios, 77
Positive reinforcement, 55
Power, 54
Practice test analysis
  chart, 127–40
  exercise, 101
Praise, effective, 64
Precocious, 16
Prejudice, 33
Preoperational stage, 37
Pretests, 61, 76
Prior knowledge, 20
Probing, 63
Problem solving, 3
  as best practice, 20
  fostering, 20
  word associations, 26
Process, learning as, 24
Productivity tools, 74
Professional development,
    86–89, 125
  activities, 2
  best practices, 86
  campus improvement plan
    (CIP), 87
  collaboration, 86
  community support, 88–89
  conduct, teacher, 87
  learner-centered, 4–5

school community, 86–87
  support resources, 87–88
Professional development
    appraisal system (PDAS), 88
Professional goals, 4
Professionalism, 5, 82
Proficiency, 16
Project learning, 16
Prominent, 50
Prompting, 63
Proximodistal development, 38
Psychomotor domain, 33, 43
Public Law (PL) 94-142
  Section 504, 91
Punishment, 55

Q
Questioning techniques, 64–65
  convergent, 65
  divergent, 65
  effective, 64–65
  skilled, 65
  wait time, 65
Questions
  dissection exercise, 10–13
  intent of, 7–8, 10
  keywords in, 8, 10
  plan, 21
  rereading, 8–9
  rewriting, 8, 10
  underlining, 7–8, 10

R
Race, 40
Rationale, 16
Reality therapy, 55
  basic needs and, 55
Reasoning
  deductive, 61
  inductive, 61
Reflection, 16, 21
  modeling, 45
  techniques, 20
Reflective teaching, 45
Reinforcement, 55
  negative, 55
  positive, 55
Reliability, 75
Rereading, of questions, 8–9
Research-based practices, 20–23
  exercise, 22–23
Resources, technological, 4
Respectful behavior, modeling, 3
Restating, 61
Rewriting, questions, 8
Right brain/hemisphere, 46

Risk taking
  as best practice, 20
  encouraging, 21
  as positive behavior, 45
Room arrangement, 57
Rote learning, 16
Rough and tumble play, 38
Rubric, 61

S
Salad bowl theory, 33
Scaffolding, 33, 37
Schema, 33
School, mission for, 4
School-community relationships,
  fostering, 20
School-home relationships,
  fostering, 20
Schools, ties with community, 4
Scope, 16
Search string, 73
Section 504, 91
Self, emergence of, 38
Self-actualization, 33
Self-assessment, 21, 45
  as best practice, 20
Self-concept, 33
Self-directed learning, 16
  encouraging, 3
Self-directed thinking, 21
Self-discipline model, 55
Self-efficacy, 33
Self-esteem, 33
Self-monitoring, 45
Sensorimotor stage, 37
Serious misbehavior, 55
Simulation, 74
Site-based decision making
  (SBDM), 87
Site-based management team
  (SBMT), 87
Skilled questioning, 65
Skinner, B.F., 55
Social development, 36, 38
Social interactions, importance
  of, 37
Social skills, goals, 70
Software, 73
  application programs, 73–74
  piracy and copyright laws,
  74–75
Solitary play, 38
Special needs, 40
  philosophy for, 10
  types of, 91–92
Sponge activity, 50

Spontaneity test, 93
Spreadsheet, 74
Standardized test, 76
  achievement test, 76
  aptitude test, 76
  criterion-referenced test, 76
  norm-referenced test, 76
Stereotype, 33
Strategies, test-taking, 7–13
Student behavior, managing,
  53–57, 119
  assertive discipline, 54
  best practices, 53
  classroom management, 53–54
  conflict resolution, 56–57
  management style, 54
  operant conditioning, 55
  problems, 55–56
  reality therapy, 55
  room arrangement, 57
Student-centered, 16
Student learning, instruction and
  assessment for, 31–48
Student ownership, 16
  of learning, 20
Students
  accountability, 21
  goals for, 3
  ownership of learning, 21
  plans for, 3
  responsibility for learning, 3
  risk-taking, 3
Student teams-achievement
  division (STAD), 68
Subjectivity, 16
Summative assessment, 61, 76
Support resources, for teachers,
  87–88
Synthesis, 43
  exercise, 102–6

T
Tactile (kinesthetic) learners, 32
Teacher-centered, 16
Teacher certification, Pedagogy
  and Professional
  Responsibilities (PPR)
  TExES
  exams and, 1
Teachers
  as advocate, 4
  as coach, 2
  collaborative team of, 5
  conduct, 87
  as critical thinker, 2
  ethical principles, 5

  as facilitator, 3
  learner-centered proficiencies
  for, 1–5
  as manager, 3
  objectives, writing, 42
  as problem solver, 2
  risk-taking, 3
  role in cooperative learning,
  69–70
  technological resources for, 4
Teacher self-report form, 88
Teaching techniques
  inquiry, 4
  media, 4
  nonverbal, 4
  verbal, 4
Teams-assisted individualization
  (TAI), 68–69
Teams-games tournament, 68
Team teaching, 86
Technological resources, for
  teachers, 4
Technology, 72–75, 122
  best practices, 72
  defined, 16
  equity in access to, 72
  software application
  programs, 73–74
  software piracy and copyright
  laws, 74–75
  terms, 72–73
  word associations, 26
Terminology, 16
Test construction, 77
  guidelines for, 77
  test items, 77
Test philosophy, 1–6
  exercise, 5
  learner-centered proficiencies
  for teachers, 1–5
Test-taking strategies, 7–13
  answers, understand intent of,
  9
  distracters, eliminating, 8
  keywords, identifying, 8
  rereading questions, 8
  rewriting questions, 8
  underlining, 7
  verbs, identifying, 9
Texas, learner-centered
  proficiencies for teachers
  in, 1
Texas Assessment of Knowledge
  and Skills (TAKS), 42
Texas Education Agency (TEA),
  1

Texas Essential Knowledge and
    Skills (TEKS), 41–42
Thinking
    creative, 20
    critical, 3, 15, 20
    higher-level, 9, 32
    higher-order, 20
    self-directed, 21
Title I, 82
Traditional lesson cycle, 43
Transition, 50
Trust *versus* mistrust stage, 38
Tutorial, 74

U
Underlining, 7–8, 10
Unit, 43

V
Validity, 75
Verbal cues, 63
Verbal teaching techniques, 4
Verbs
    common, 28–29
    identifying, 9
Vertical teaming, 86
Vicarious learning, 16
Vocabulary
    for domain I, PPR, 32–35
    for domain II, PPR, 50–51
    for domain III, PPR, 61–62
    for domain IV, PPR, 82–83
    exercise, 34–35
Vygotsky, Lev, 37

W
Wait time, in questioning, 65
Webcam, 73
Wide area network (WAN), 73
Word associations, 26–27
Word processing, 74
Writing
    objectives, 42
    word processing and, 74

Z
Zero reject, 89
Zone of proximal development
    (ZPD), 33, 37